FEATURES OF THIS BOOK

- 490 entries in this unique book

- Descriptions and full-color illustrations and photographs of most recognized breeds

- Descriptions and prognosis of all common cat diseases and ailments, their prevention and treatment

- Practical information on choosing and caring for a cat, feeding and traveling

- History and lore of the cat, superstitions and sayings

- Entries on the cat in art, literature and religion

The Dell

Encyclopedia of

CATS

by Barbara Shook Hazen

Illustrated by Roy Wiltshire
with additional drawings by
Paul Singer

This book is dedicated to Caesar
who always knew it all,
and to Machias and Mouser
for their paws' worth.

Published by
Delacorte Press.

An original work created and produced by
Vineyard Books, Inc.
159 East 64 Street
New York, New York 10021

Delacorte ® TM 823663, Dell Publishing Co., Inc.
Printed in Italy by Arnoldo Mondadori Editore, Sp A

ISBN 0-440-01764-5

INTRODUCTION

This book is intended as a concise, informative, helpful and, we hope, entertaining compendium of the cat. It is meant for the long-time cat owner and lover, and for someone newly toying with the idea of taking up with a cat.

The entries are arranged in compact, easy-to-find alphabetical form. They include illustrations and detailed descriptions of all the standard breeds. Cat shows and cats in different countries are discussed for those who are interested. Likewise, cat lore: the cat in art, literature, history, religion and superstition. All the medical and practical aspects of owning a cat are included, from whisker to tail tip, Abrasions to Zoopsychology. In other words, this is meant to be a sound, helpful, factual yet flexible manual. It should aid in handling any emergency or dealing with any idiosyncracy. It should help you care for and get closer to your cat and increase an appreciation of all cats.

Special thanks go to Pres Bowles, true cat lover and swift manuscript runner, Dr. Benjamin Schulberg, wise veterinarian down the block, who has given liberal doses of humor, insight and help, and all city and country cats who have charmed and enlightened me along the way. And my most special thanks to Julius Caesar, my secretary-tabby, who has uncomplainingly commented, shuffled and sat on so much of the manuscript. To him I owe an important insight: that no matter what is said in these pages, some cat somewhere will refute it. Because to a large degree feline philosophy can be summed up categorically: Whatever works is.

BARBARA SHOOK HAZEN

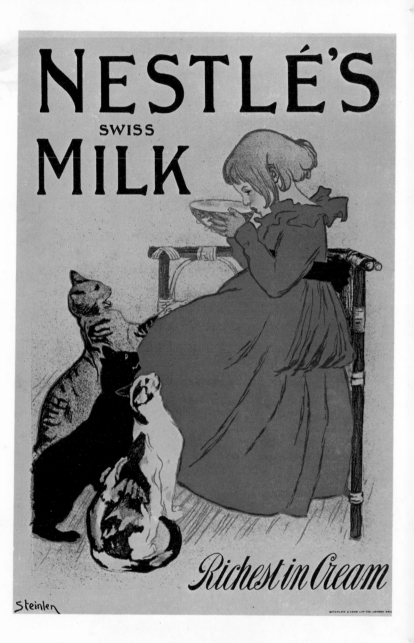

A

ABRASION: a sore, scraped spot often caused by rubbing against a rough object. Simple abrasions are best treated by white petroleum jelly, mineral oil, or any mild non-toxic ointment. If the sore does not heal, see your veterinarian, who will likely prescribe an *antibiotic*.

ABSCESS: a localized collection of pus which forms around germs or a *foreign body*, and which may usually be felt as a lump. An abscessed area is likely to be swollen and feel warm. Do not squeeze the abscess, though as a temporary measure you may put compresses of warm salt water on the area. Abscesses are most often caused by rat bites or bites from other cats or by imbedded objects. They are extremely dangerous and painful to cats. See your veterinarian.

ABYSSINIAN: a slender, elegant, short-haired cat supposedly descended from ancient cats of Egypt. Abyssinians are powerful

This brown Abyssinian kitten seems to be whispering in mother's ear.

Abyssinian

and graceful. They have long tails, triangular faces, and distinctively ticked fur—that is, each hair is banded and tipped with black. The most frequently seen Abyssinian,

Red Abyssinian

is a ruddy brown color with black ticking and black foot pads. It has large expressive green, yellow, or hazel eyes and prominent ears.

A second variety, the red Abyssinian, lacks any black pigment and has a brick red coat ticked with darker red and brown, and pink foot pads. Still a third variety, the cream Abyssinian, is being bred but is not yet recognized.

As pets, Abyssinians are affectionate and devoted. Unlike many cats, they are fond of water. An oddity of the breed is that more males than females are born.

ACCIDENTS: unexpected, undesirable happenings to cats. The most common accident is being hit by a car. Have the cat checked by a veterinarian even if there is no obvious external sign of injury. Move the cat as little as possible, handle it gently and cover it to prevent *shock*.

Cats also fall from time to time, and while a cat may fall from an amazing height and not be hurt, this is not always true. Have your cat checked, if it falls from a distance, if it has trouble moving, or if it is obviously injured. Otherwise, keep the cat quiet and in a confined place. Don't feed it for the rest of the day. Afterwards, if it doesn't eat, take it to the veterinarian; it is likely there are internal injuries. (See also: *bites, broken bones, burns* and *cuts*.)

ACCOMODATION OF PUPILS: the unique ability of the cat's pupils to contract and expand to adjust to the available amount of light. In near darkness, the pupil is round and wide; in bright sunlight, it is a thin slit.

ACID MILK: an acid condition in the mother cat's milk which causes the kittens to stop *nursing* or to vomit immediately afterwards. Milk of magnesia given to the mother cat is commonly said to be a cure, though not all experts agree.

ACQUIRING A CAT OR KITTEN: If you decide to get a cat or kitten from a pet shop or directly from a *breeder*, check his reputation first. An old saying is never to buy a cat from any place that smells of cat (which indicates sickness). Specify that you want to be able to return the cat if it doesn't pass a veterinarian examination within a specified time. Go directly to the breeder to get a top quality *pedigreed* cat. If you're not sure

A cat's pupil contracts in bright light

and expands in semi-darkness.

Her first kitten!

9

Two is company; true of kittens as well as children.

what kind, shop around at the cat shows, where you can also get the names and addresses of good breeders. Keep in mind that certain breeds have certain problems, for instance *long-haired cats* must be groomed daily for good health and good looks.

If you just want a cat or kitten that wants you, choose one from friends or adopt a cat from one of the reputable animal agencies such as the *A.S.P.C.A.*, which often give shots and health check-ups before selling. (Some also make the new owner promise to *alter* the cat.)

When choosing a kitten, pick one at least eight or nine weeks old. If it doesn't have two rows of clean, sharp *teeth*, it's too young. Ditto if it isn't completely weaned. Check its general health and vivacity. Sometimes the *runt* of the litter

is the brightest and most active. Warning signals are rashes and scaly patches, skimpy fur, a hard, swollen belly (often a sign of *worms*), evidence of *diarrhea* (wetness around the tail), and general unresponsiveness. A kitten that acts shy or unresponsive probably isn't up to par.

If you are adopting an older cat, consider that you are acquiring a pet with a known health record and a known disposition, which may be ideal if you have very young or very rambunctious children. If you are adopted by a *stray*, take it for a veterinary check-up before it settles in. If it's hopelessly sick, you'll want to know before you are hopelessly attached to it.

Whether cat or kitten, when you are acquiring a pet from a former owner, take notes about its previous care, food and meal schedule, any illnesses and operations and shots received.

Other considerations being equal, stick with your instinctive first choice, the cat or kitten that undoubtedly chose you.

ADOPTION BY A FOSTER MOTHER: A *nursing* mother cat (*queen*) will sometimes accept strange kittens, or even puppies or rabbits, especially if they are near the same age as her own kittens. The trick is to collect some of the mother's own milk and rub the strange kittens with it. Then put them in the cat basket while the mother cat is away. If they smell like her milk, she is more likely to accept them when she returns.

AFFECTION: Warm, fond feelings are commonly shown in cats by purring (sometimes accompanied by *drooling*), *kneading*, rubbing, and, of course, lap sitting. (See also *behavior*.)

AFRICAN WILD CAT: a nocturnal Asian and African cat, somewhat larger than the domestic cat, with a *tabby* coat pattern, ringed tail and yellowish belly. It mates with domestic cats when given the opportunity. Some say it is a relative of the *European Wild Cat*.

AFTERBIRTH: the mass, including the placenta, expelled after birth. It is medically important that each kitten be followed by its afterbirth.

Cats and children make natural, close and caring companions.

Albino

AGE: see *life span*.

AGING CATS AND THEIR CARE: Old age in the cat begins at about nine or ten years. An older cat should be treated with special dignity, gentleness, and affection. Particular attention should be given to *diet, teeth*, and general *health*. Provide a comfortable, draft-free bed and see that the cat gets regular exercise. Older cats are prone to *constipation, kidney troubles, arthritis*, and *colds*.

AILUROPHILE: someone who loves cats. Famous ailurophiles include Abraham Lincoln, Albert Einstein, Colette, T. S. Eliot, and Winston Churchill, whose cat often accompanied him to cabinet meetings. Another famous cat lover was Mohammed, who once cut off the bottom part of his robe rather than disturb his pet cat.

AILUROPHOBE: one who has an intense and morbid dislike of cats. Some famous tyrants, among them Julius Caesar, Alexander the Great, and Mussolini, were known

ailurophobes. Napoleon was said to break out in a cold sweat at the sight of the smallest kitten.

AIR: Fresh air is invigorating and good for cats. Stale, polluted, or dusty air can cause respiratory problems. Paint fumes are particularly dangerous, as are the fumes from many insect sprays.

ALBINO: a cat born without pigmentation, without the gene for color development. Genuine albino domestic cats are rare. They have white hair and pink eyes. There is an albino strain in Tigers.

ALLERGIES, CAT: states of hypersensitivity in the cat to certain drugs, such as penicillin, insects, such as *fleas*, and foods. Symptoms include inflammation, skin rash and reddening, and respiratory problems. Allergic reactions in the cat range from mild to fatal. Treatment is by antihistamines and other drugs. See your *veterinarian*.

ALLERGY, HUMAN TO CAT: Humans sometimes have allergic reactions to cat hair and dander, resulting in wheezing, sneezing, itching, and *asthma*. Treatment by drugs and serum desensitization is generally effective, but varies according to the individual.

ALLEY CAT: a disparaging term to describe any cat of mixed parentage.

ALOOFNESS: an aspect of cats' independent and innately reserved nature, often mistaken for disdain by dog lovers.

ALOPECIA: a condition in which the cat progressively loses its hair in patches. Hormone treatment by a *veterinarian* sometimes helps.

His lack of pedigree doesn't keep the alley cat from being one of the most beautiful animals alive.

ALTERING: a term which technically means the neutering of either a male or female cat, but which is commonly applied to the neutering of the male. It is a safe surgical operation which should be done while the animal is young, around six months, to prevent the development of secondary sex characteristics: aggressiveness, straying in search of a female, and the *spraying* of strong smelling urine. Simple sterilization, vasectomy, without the removal of the testicles does not alter the offensive-to-humans sexual characteristics. Nor is the operation as successful in the adult cat as it is in the kitten. An altered cat is just as playful and may be even more affectionate. Certainly he is less likely to roam and get in cat fights, though certain sexual characteristics, such as *kneading*, are retained. There is no medical proof that an altered cat is more likely to get fat or to develop bladder stones. (See also *spaying*.)

AMERICA, CATS IN: Real interest in cat breeding and showing began in the United States with a cat show of 176 cats held at Madison Square Garden in 1895. It was staged by an Englishman who had been to the earlier Crystal Palace show. In 1899, the first *cat club* was formed, soon followed by others. Today there are a number of important cat clubs and associations giving shows and setting standards, but there is no one gov-

A veteran champion, this Short-Haired Silver Tabby takes its many ribbons and congratulatory messages in stride.

erning authority as in Britain. Today there are more *pedigreed* cats in the United States than in any other country, and cats, their care, and feeding, are a multi-million dollar business. America is also active in breeding—the *Burmese* cat was developed in the States.

AMERICAN BLUE: see *Russian Blue*.

AMERICAN SHORT-HAIR: see *Domestic Short-Hair*.

AMERICAN STANDARDS: the characteristics that would be ideal for the different breeds and varieties of cat in American cat shows. There are two main divisions: short-hairs and long-hairs.

There are many sub-divisions including the different breeds and the different classes (male or female or *neuter* or *kitten*). In the United States the situation is complicated by the fact that there is no one all-governing cat authority. Rather there are a number of different associations, sometimes disagreeing on what they consider a classification. For instance, the National Cat Fanciers' Association includes the *Red Point Siamese* as a *Siamese,* while some other associations refer to them as *Colorpoints*.

The points for a perfect specimen in any category always add up to 100. Note the following scales of points for three popular

STANDARDS *(most popular American breeds)*

DOMESTIC SHORT HAIR

Head: broad between ears, cheeks well developed, face and nose shortish — 10

Ears: medium-sized, round at tips, not too broad at base — 5

Eye Opening: round — 5

Body: well knit, powerful, full chest — 15

Tail: proportionate to body, rather thick at base, tapering to tip — 5

Legs and Feet: in proportion; feet rounded, five toes in front, four in back — 10

Coat: short, lustrous, good texture — 15

Color: according to standard color and marking standards — 25

Eye Color: conforming to coat color — 5

General Condition: — 5

————
100

PERSIAN*

Color: according to standard — 25

Coat: long, glossy, standing away from body, long, curved ear tufts, full tail, ruff, and frill — 15

Condition: — 10

Head: round and massive, wide skull, shortish neck; round, full, wide-set eyes — 20

Type: includes body shape, which should be cobby, low on legs, deep in chest, massive over shoulders and rump; short, uncurved tail — 20

Eye Color: to conform with coat — 10

————
100

SIAMESE

Head: long, narrowing to muzzle, seen as wedge-shaped from front, flat skull (Roundness is undesirable). Three points for profile, five for wedge, two for chin — 10

Type: alert, rather large ears, wide at base (five points); slightly almond-shaped eyes (ten points); medium, long, lithe body (seven points); long, slender neck (three points); narrow, long tail tapering to tip, no visible kink (five points); hind legs slightly higher than front legs, largish, round feet (five points) — 45

Coat: short, fine, glossy, close to body — 10

Eye Color: clear, brilliant deep blue — 10

Body Color: even, with darker shading across shoulders and back, lighter shading on belly and chest (somewhat darker color allowed for older cats, lighter for kittens) — 10

Points: mask, ears, legs, and tail clearly defined in darker shade (except in kittens); any bars on tail, light hairs in points are objections — 15

Condition: — 10

————
100

*Note: in tabby and tortoiseshell Persians, the alotted 25 points for color are divided to give 15 for markings and 10 for color.

breeds (which may vary slightly by association). It will be seen that certain attributes are more important in one breed though the major breakdown into type, coat, and color and so forth is similar. Thus color in the *Persian* standard is worth the same number of points as color and points in the *Siamese* standard. Table 1.

AMPUTATION: the surgical removal of a limb due to accident or disease. The chances of adjustment in the cat are good.

ANAL GLANDS: two small bean-sized glands containing a secretion thought to aid in the identification of one cat by another. Only occasionally do they become impacted or abscessed in cats. See your veterinarian.

ANATOMY: the structure of the cat's body and the relation of the various parts and systems to each other. It includes the alimentary, respiratory, urinary, and nervous systems, plus the joints, muscles, and sense organs.

Parts of Cat 1. *Ear* **2.** *Forehead* **3.** *Nose* **4.** *Nostrils* **5.** *Neck* **6.** *Shoulder* **7.** *Nape* **8.** *Back* **9.** *Ribs* **10.** *Flank* **11.** *Loins* **12.** *Hip* **13.** *Hindquarters* **14.** *Tail* **15.** *Thigh* **16.** *Rump* **17.** *Shank* **18.** *Heel* **19.** *Metatarsus* **20.** *Lips* **21.** *Shoulder Blade* **22.** *Fore Leg* **23.** *Wrist* **24.** *Metacarpus* **25.** *Toes* **26.** *Elbow* **27.** *Belly* **28.** *Knee* **29.** *Hind Toes*

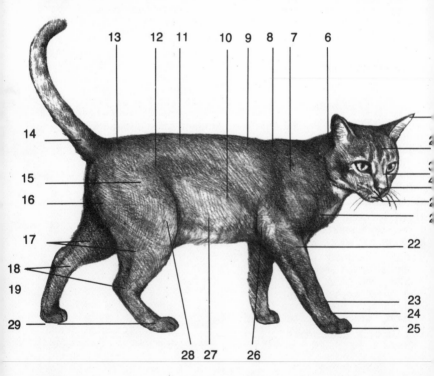

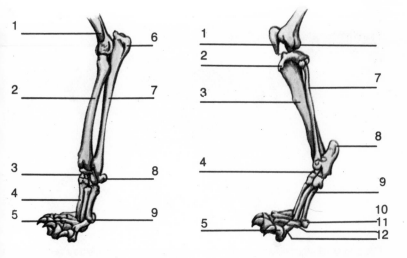

Front Leg 1. *Humerus* **2.** *Radius* **3.** *Carpus* **4.** *Metacarpus* **5.** *Phalanx Prima* **6.** *Olecranon* **7.** *Ulna* **8.** *Os Pisforme* **9.** *Sesamoid Bones*

Rear Leg 1. *Patella* **2.** *Tibia Swelling* **3.** *Tibia* **4.** *Tarsus* **5.** *Phalanx Tertia* **6.** *Os Femoris* **7.** *Fibula* **8.** *Tuber Calanei* **9.** *Metatarsus* **10.** *Sesamoid Bones* **11.** *Phalanx Prima* **12.** *Phalanx Tertia*

Internal Organs. 1. *Spinal Cord* **2.** *Cerebellum* **3.** *Cerebrum* **4.** *Kidney* **5.** *Spleen* **6.** *Tongue* **7.** *Lungs* **8.** *Trachea* **9.** *Esophagus* **10.** *Heart* **11.** *Liver* **12.** *Stomach* **13.** *Intestine* **14.** *Bladder* **15.** *Rectum.*

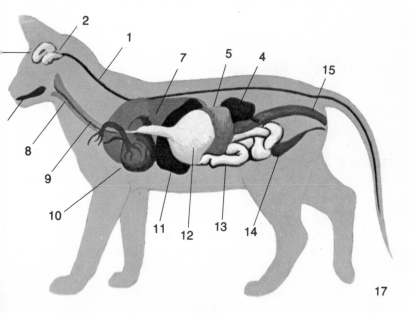

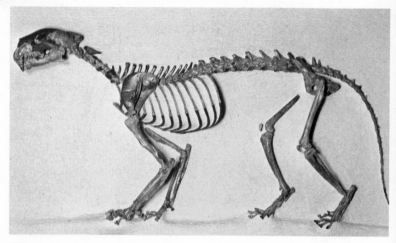

The sleek, elongated shape of the modern day cat can clearly be seen in this skeleton of the ancient Dinitis.

ANCESTORS OF THE CAT: The ancestors of the cat have not been definitely identified. Generally the cat is traced back to Miacis (also considered the ancestor of the dog), a weasel-like carnivore that existed about 50 million years ago. It had short legs, a long body, and a vicious nature.

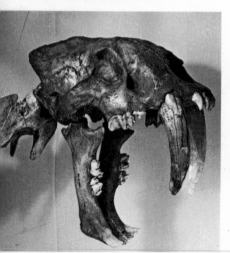

The cat evidently descended from Miacis through the Civet, about 40 million years ago—a rather abrupt process as evolutionary processes go, and 10 to 20 million years before the dog appeared. Dr. Edwin H. Colbert of the American Museum of Natural History states that "One might say that certain Civets jumped into the roles of cats with all the evolutionary rapidity of a quick-change artist in a hard-pressed double part."

The first cats were divided into two groups: *Hoplophoneus* and *Dinictis*. The former, sometimes called *Smilodon*, were lion-sized and large bodied and had long saber-like canine teeth, all the better for felling the huge, lumbering beasts on the earth in those prehistoric times. When these beasts

A fossil skull typical of the Smilodon group.

18

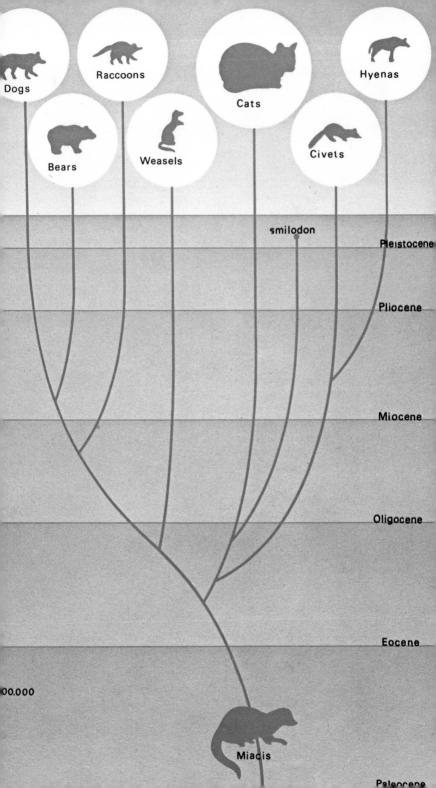

Dogs

Raccoons

Bears

Weasels

Cats

Civets

Hyenas

smilodon

Pleistocene

Pliocene

Miocene

Oligocene

Eocene

00.000

Miacis

Paleocene

began to die out, so did the saber-toothed *Smilodon* as it was too large and clumsy to catch smaller, more agile animals.

The second group, *Dinictis*, was the forerunner of our modern cat. These smaller animals were fast, graceful, and highly adaptable, with teeth well designed for killing and eating, and an alert intelligence. Today's cat remains relatively unchanged from the specimens of *Dinictis* found in ancient fossils.

ANEMIA: a reduction in the number of normal red blood cells, a condition not uncommon in cats, particularly older ones. Symptoms include weakness, pale, sore gums, and breathlessness. Anemia may be caused by internal bleeding, vitamin deficiency, *worms*, or disease. Consult with your veterinarian.

ANESTHESIA: any medicine or agent which makes the cat patient unaware of pain. Local anesthetics affect only a particular part of the body; general anesthetics cause total temporary unconsciousness.

ANGORA: a name formerly used for long-haired cats of the *Persian* type. It is not regarded as a distinct breed anymore, though some people still claim that Angoras are different from Persian Cats, having silkier coats, smaller heads, and longer noses and bodies.

ANTIBIOTICS: a family of potent drugs including penicillin, made from molds and bacteria and used in the treatment of disease and infection. Should be used only as directed and only under veterinary supervision.

ANTIHISTAMINES: medicines used chiefly to treat respiratory and skin disorders of an allergic nature.

ANTISEPTICS: Salves and solutions used to keep minor cuts and scratches germ free and to prevent festering. The affected surface should be cleaned before applying the antiseptic. Diluted hydrogen peroxide is an effective yet gentle antiseptic for cats. Mild ointments are also good. If in doubt about a product, consult with your veterinarian. (See also *disinfectants*.)

ANY OTHER COLOR: a classification at cat shows for quality cats that don't conform to any set breed standard.

APPETITE: desire for food. In the cat appetite may be adversely affected by psychological factors such as *jealousy*, removal to strange surroundings, a disliking of a particular food, illness, a *hairball*, or a whim. Most cats do go "off feed" from time to time, or change in their food whims. If the cat also seems listless or if nothing tempts it, call your veterinarian

ART, CATS IN: Aesthetically the cat was first discovered by the Egyptians, Japanese, Chinese and Incas. It was a long time later (the sixteenth and seventeenth centuries) that the cat appeared in European art. Leonardo da Vinci beautifully drew cats, and cats began to appear in religious art,

Since then, in diverse styles and manners, the cat has been rendered in painting, sculpture and illustration by numerous artists including Hogarth, Manet, Renoir, Chagall, Steinberg and Picasso.

An Egyptian wall painting. Note hunting cat (under elbow).

In this Egyptian wall painting a pet cat patiently awaits for tidbits of food to fall under its mistress's chair during a banquet.

Below, a Roman mosaic depicts a cat devouring a partridge.

At left, a cat stalks a partridge under a banquet table in this early Roman fresco.

Below, a cat and dog share scraps in this detail from a painting, The Last Supper, by Lorenzetti.

This 15th Century Persian miniature shows the age-old tradition of a cat chasing a mouse.

17th Century Persian earthenware bottle in the shape of a cat.

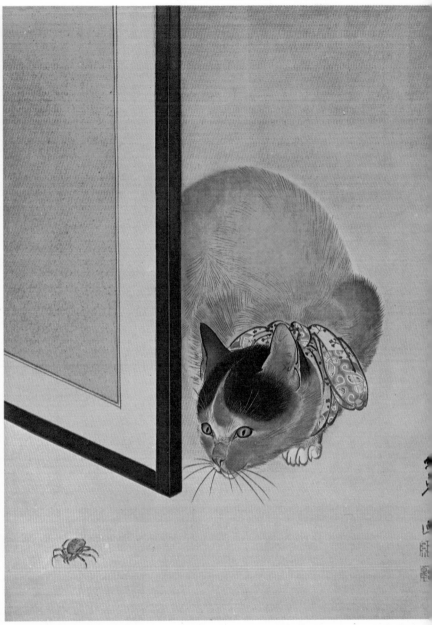

A cat stalks a spider in this contemporary Japanese painting.

A Western Chinese child's cotton apron. 19th Century.

A Persian bronze incense burner in the shape of a cat.

The attraction of cat for bird is eloquently shown in this painting by
William Hogarth.

A steel engraving by Gustave Doré, 1839, shows Puss in Boots holding
court.

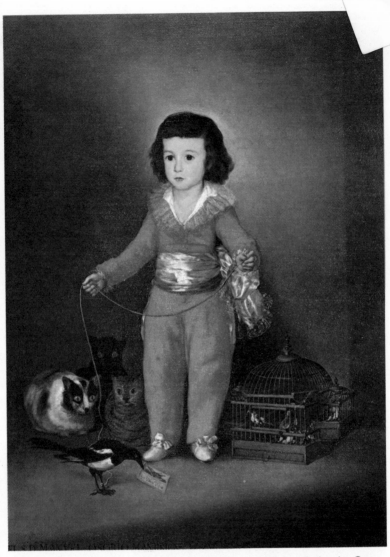

Plump cats observe a pet bird in this famous Spanish painting by Goya.

A Persian appears on this French Wallpaper, printed from wood blocks. ca. 1840.

Two Cats, a black and white drawing by Giovanni Tiepolo.

This comfortable cat and reflective woman were painted by Edward Manet.

A French black and white woodcut, Indolence, *by Felix Vallotton, 1896*

This drawing of Fritsi, is by Paul Klee, 1919.

An early American painting titled Tinkle, A Cat.

A sleek sculptured bronze by Duncan Ferguson, 1928.

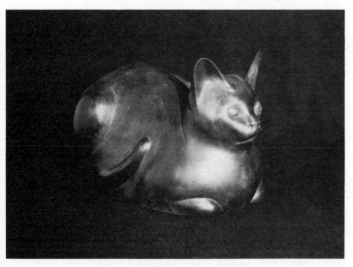

Angora Cat *by Morris Hirschfield.*

A bigger-than-life cat is seen in a painting by Richard Lindner.

The cat shown in this painting by Fernando Botero greatly resembles the group surrounding it. The painting is titled The Presidential Family.

WHAT HAVE I DONE TO
DESERVE ALL THESE KITTENS.

Herriman

The famous Chaplin-like Mehitabel drawn by the cartoonist George Herriman.

ARTHRITIS: inflammation of a joint. Luckily it occurs rarely in cats, though it may be caused by animal bites which have penetrated the joint. Rest and antibiotics may help. See your veterinarian.

ARTIFICIAL RESPIRATION: a means of starting normal breathing again after near *drowning, gas poisoning,* or *electric shock.* (If the cat has been in water, first hold it up by the hind legs and let the water drain out of the mouth.)

There are several methods. The simplest is to put the cat between your knees and put your hands on the cat's sides behind the shoulder. Press gently but firmly (severe pressure can cause injury) every two or three seconds.

A second method is to use mouth to mouth resuscitation after first clearing the mouth of water and pulling the tongue to the side. Tilt the cat's head back. Take a deep breath, place your mouth over the cat's mouth and exhale just hard enough so that the cat's sides rise. Do this about 25 times a minute.

Still a third method is to hold the cat by its tail and swing it back and forth in a regular, smooth motion to the count of four.

A.S.P.C.A.: initials which stand for the American Society for the Prevention of Cruelty to Animals, an institution founded in 1865 and fashioned after the similar British Association. The society emphasizes responsible pet ownership and humane treatment of all animals. It investigates alleged cruelty to animals, urges the passage of humane laws, and finds homes for lost and abandoned pets. (Anyone who adopts a cat from the A.S.P.C.A. must promise to have the animal neutered and has 72 hours in which to exchange the pet if it doesn't pass a veterinary check-up.) The A.S.P.C.A. also gives medical aid and helps in the disposal of deceased pets.

ASPIRIN: proprietary name for acetylsalicylic acid, a common drug given for reducing pain and lowering temperature. Regular aspirin should never be given to cats; it makes them gag and is highly toxic. More palatable baby aspirin (1¼ gram) may be used, under veterinary supervision.

ASTHMA: an allergic condition characterized by wheezing and other breathing difficulties. Rare in cats, but repeated attacks can damage the lungs permanently. Veterinary attention is needed.

ATAVISM: the reappearance in kittens of characteristics belonging to a more or less remote ancestor, or traits which have skipped several generations. This is why, in breeding, it is important to examine as many ancestors as possible.

ATROPHY: the shrinking of an unused organ, such as a leg, from lack of use, often following a fracture. The situation usually solves itself when the limb is used again.

AUSTRALIA, CATS IN: There is no one central governing cat association in Australia, rather each state has its own organization. There is a great interest in breeding and showing, and the breeds, for the most part, follow the British standards.

AUSTRALIAN BLUE: another name for a short-haired Blue cat.

AUSTRALIAN CAT: a now extinct breed of cat that supposedly mutated from a *Siamese* cat introduced into Australia near the end of the nineteenth century. They had odd, squirrel-like heads, were delicate and produced such small litters that they soon died out.

AUTOPSY: a post-mortem examination to determine the cause of death. While sometimes distressing to an owner, permitting an autopsy of a dead cat may help in the treatment of living cats with similar problems.

AUTUMN LITTERS: litters born of *queens* who were in season in late summer. The only disadvantage is in raising kittens during colder weather.

B

BABIES AND CATS: Cats generally love babies. Even jealous cats tend to sulk rather than harm the new arrival. However, a cat could accidently harm a tiny infant, so it is best not to leave a cat alone in a room with a very small baby. Cats and older children make natural companions.

BABY FOOD: good, nourishing alternate food for cats, especially young cats and cats with tooth or

Cats and small children have a special kind of understanding.

digestive troubles. Liver and beef are particularly nourishing.

BAD BREATH: To a certain extent a cat's breath depends on what it eats; it will smell fishy if it eats mostly fish. Really foul breath, however, is a symptom of ill health—tooth decay, abscess, kidney failure or intestinal trouble. Have cat the checked out by your veterinarian.

BALDNESS: From time to time *breeders* have tried to develop strains of nearly bald cats. Plucked-looking and unattractive, they do not appeal to most cat lovers. Some established breeds, such as the *Devon Rex,* are prone to baldness because of their very fragile down hairs.

Temporary baldness sometimes results from *mange*, illness, *hormone* imbalance, or a bad *diet*, while severe *burns* and senility sometimes result in permanent bald patches. Rub olive or other oil on the dry skin area if it cracks or is excessively dry.

BALINESE: a variety of North American cat with *Siamese* markings that is sometimes called the Long-Haired Siamese. The breed supposedly arose from *mutation.* A kitten with an unusually long coat was born into a litter of Siamese. Similar kittens appeared in other litters, and these, mated to each other, bred true.

The characteristic type, shape, coloring, and markings are Siamese. The only difference is that the coat is two or so inches long. *Persian* characteristics are considered a fault in this unusually attractive and intelligent variety.

BANDAGING: A cat may have to be bandaged when injured to keep it from scratching itself. The procedure is often difficult and it is a good idea to have an assistant to help hold the cat. Any bandage should be flat and firm, but not so tight it interferes with circulation. Use tape rather than pins to secure the bandage and bandage the whole area, not just the injured part. There are special stocking bandages for paws.

After bandaging, most cats are desperate to pull the bandage off. Sometimes putting *butter* on an unhurt paw will distract a cat, who tries to lick the butter off rather than pull the bandage off. (See also *cardboard collar.)*

BASKETS: see *carrying cases.*

BATHS: Cats bathe themselves instinctively and well. (The only

Balinese

39

"I'd rather do it myself" is the attitude of most cats toward an enforced tub bath.

place a cat cannot reach by a combination of paw and tongue is in between its shoulder blades.)

In an emergency—*fleas, lice,* or a smelly mess the cat has fallen into—bathe the cat with mild soap or special pet shampoo. Do not use harsh detergents. Do groom the cat first; water will make any snarls worse.

Two tubs are a help, one for soaping and one for rinsing. An alternative is to place the cat head out in some kind of porous bag. Dunk the bag into the soapy water and pat the cat.

Protect the cat's ears with cotton, and its eyes with a drop of mineral oil or petroleum jelly. Rinse

and dry thoroughly. Avoid drafts. Some cats love to be fluff-dried by hairdryers.

There are also special commercial powders for dry cleaning cats, and spot cleaning can be done with a damp sponge or washcloth.

BEDS: Any cat bed, whether a fancy store-bought one or a converted cardboard box, should be large enough so the cat can stretch comfortably and should be enclosed on three sides. Place it in a draft-free spot, preferably off the floor. Put newspaper on the bottom to conserve heat and a washable blanket or towel on top for cosiness.

Special stationary beds are only a necessity for invalid cats, young kittens, and pregnant *queens*. Most cats prefer to pick their own sleeping place, varying it according to climate and whim.

BEHAVIOR, NORMAL: Above all cats are independent, individualistic, and mysterious. Almost everything that can be said about one cat can be contradicted by another. However, there are some general behavior patterns.

A cat is a loner, a hunter, and a highly territorial animal. It tends to mark off its own space and is not a pack animal, as a dog is.

It is always wary of an approaching strange cat. (On the other hand, kittens are highly sociable, two adult cats in the same household often become close companions, and groups of stray cats tend to gather for purely social reasons.)

Cats are highly sexual creatures. Unaltered males battle for domination and female favors; females make tender, caring mothers (except for the few mother cats who ignore their kittens). Cats are highly adaptable to circumstance yet they are fastidious lovers of creature comforts. Often an adopted, ratty-looking alley cat, once ensconced inside, turns out

The pouncing game is one that the cat plays best.

to be the pet that wants the most pampering, the one that prefers the silk spread.

Cats are affectionate, but not necessarily when you want them to be, and often the affection is more a subtle respect than the pawing kind of display dogs give.

No creature can relax more completely than the cat and no creature has more nervous energy. Cats are ferocious and tender, loving and disinterested, creatures of habit and creatures of whim—most cats combine all of these traits.

In instinctive behavior, there is a greater degree of consistency. *Kneading* soft objects with the front paws, cleaning with the *tongue, claw* sharpening, arching the back when wanting to appear threatening, chasing moving objects, *calling* in the unaltered female and urine *spraying* in the altered male are things that all cats do and all do differently. Often domestic cats act more individually than instinctively. For instance, many chase mice more for sport than for eating, often carrying them proudly as trophies to their owners, while one well-known New York veterinarian has a cat that doesn't chase mice at all. It faints at the sight of them.

BEHAVIOR, ABNORMAL: Because cats are highly-tuned, sensitive creatures, they often act adversely to illness, moving, and other stress. A cat may chew on things because it is exasperated, lose its appetite in an owner's absence, or lapse in *housebreaking* at the introduction of a new pet or baby. Mild symptoms are likely to go away spontaneously with gentle, affectionate handling. Serious symptoms such as *fits* and wild or erratic behavior should prompt you to call your veterinarian. He may want to check your pet or prescribe a tranquilizer. In still other instances, because cats are such individualists, an animal may act in a way that is strange to us but

There's something fishy about this kitten's curiosity!

Cats are not normally mean or destructive despite the goings-on in this early engraving.

George Cruikshank

logical to the cat, as when a mother cat adopts a duckling or, on the other hand, ignores her own kittens. There are many kinds of cats and many things man doesn't know about how a cat's mind works.

BELLS: sometimes used by cat owners to prevent bird catching and to identify the whereabouts of the cat.

BI-COLORED CATS: British term for cats having white and any solid

The bird doesn't always get the worst of it: witness this cat being given a good dressing down.

other color in clear, evenly distributed patches, with not more than half the coat white. They are also called Parti-colored. Black and white combinations are sometimes called Magpies.

BIRDS AND CATS: Cats instinctively dart after any moving object including birds. If an outdoor cat catches and wounds a bird, kill the bird humanely, but do not scold the cat. Cats do not make fine moral distinctions. Belling the cat may help though some cats learn to stalk without jangling the bell. Indoor cats may be discouraged from going near bird cages by the repeated and adroit use of a water pistol. In one scientific study of cats accidently killed on the road, not one was found to have bird remains in its stomach, which shows that cats kill fewer birds than cat-haters think.

BIRMAN: Also called the Sacred Cat of Burma, this is an exotic cat once worshipped in Burmese temples, where the temple priests thought they were reincarnations of deceased and godly people. Birmans are still relatively rare in England and in the States, though they have been an established breed in France since 1952.

The Birman has a long, silky coat with a heavy *ruff* around the neck. The coat is of a *Siamese* pattern: solid body color and contrasting blue, chocolate, frost or seal *points*. The head is full and wide, the body stocky and the tail long but bushy; eyes should be blue. The most unusual feature of the breed is that the four paws are white, ending in an even line across the third joint, which gives the effect of white stockings. Also, though the fur is long, it does not mat easily.

Birman

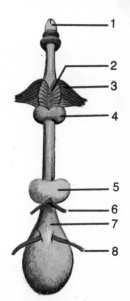

Male Generative Organ 1. *Glanis Penis* **2.** *Accelerator Urinae muscle* **3.** *Ischio-cavernosus muscle* **4.** *Cowpers gland* **5.** *Prostrate* **6.** *Vas Deferens* **7.** *Bladder* **8.** *Ureter*

BIRTH: The process of kittening. Just before giving birth, the mother cat may lose her appetite, act restless and aloof, start nest building, and have a temperature drop of one or two degrees.

BITES BY OTHER ANIMALS: Animal bites are always serious. The danger of infection is great because the puncture wounds produced by fangs are likely to be deep. *Antiseptic* applied to the surface isn't enough. It is best to call your veterinarian.

Swelling or a hard lump may be a sign of an animal bite.

BLACK CATS, BREEDS: There are purebred long-haired and short-haired black cats, however orange-eyed, jet black cats are

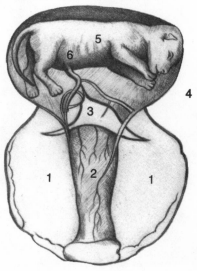

1. *Chorion* **2.** *Zonary Placenta* **3.** *Umbilical Vesicle* **4.** *Sac of Amnion* **5.** *Fetus* **6.** *Umbilical cord.*

45

rare. Often there are faint *tabby* markings, some white hairs, a rusty cast to the coat, or a green rim to the eye color—all of which are faults in a show cat. In kittens, the rusy cast and faint tabby lines sometimes disappear; sometimes not. Pure raven black is a difficult color to breed consistently.

BLACK CATS, SAYINGS AND SUPERSTITIONS: During the Middle Ages black cats were thought to have an evil eye, and black cats figured prominently in black magic recipes to cast spells and make people disappear. One still occasionally hears that trouble follows a black cat crossing in front of one or coming into the house.

On the other hand, a large number of people believe that a black cat brings good fortune, and also, that anyone who finds the one perfect, pure white hair in an all-black cat and plucks it out without being scratched will find great wealth and have good luck in love.

A black cat in the audience on opening night portends a successful play.

White cats are considered wise and lucky—or is that a lot a monkey business? asks a friend.

BLACK-FOOTED CAT: a smallish African Wild Cat with a tawny brown coat and white undersides which resembles and mates with the domestic cat. The head and shoulders are striped; the body spotted. The soles of the feet are black (the origin of its name).

BLADDER: the internal organ that holds urine, which in the cat is subject to disorders. Cats that don't get enough exercise and males are particularly prone to bladder trouble. The two most common kinds are: cystitis, which is an inflammation of the bladder, causing painful, strained urination (symptoms include blood-tinged urine, stiff hindquarters, and a pronounced ammonia odor); and bladder stones, which block the urinary passage (symptoms are a distended bladder and an inability to urinate). Consult with a veterinarian without delay, before

47

Blue-Cream Short-Hair

there are secondary complications.

BLAZE: term for a contrasting stripe or mark going from the forehead to the cat's nose.

BLEEDING: see *hemorrhage*.

BLUE-CREAM LONG-HAIR: Ideally the two colors in this variety, blue and cream, are equally divided. In America well-defined patches are preferred while in England and Europe, this is considered a fault and it is desired that the colors be softly intermingled.

Heads should be broad; eyes orange or copper. Blue-Cream Long-Hairs are invariably females.

BLUE-CREAM SHORT-HAIR: As in the long-haired variety, American and Canadian standards prefer equal patching of colors while in England and Europe an intermingling is preferred.

Blue-Cream Short-Haired cats are almost always females; males are exceedingly rare and are always sterile. (See also *Blue-Cream Long-Hair*.)

BLUE CROSS: an animal welfare organization in the United Kingdom.

BLUE PERSIAN: one of the most popular long-hairs, a variety greatly improved by selective breeding, said to result from the mating of blacks with whites. Round, deep orange eyes are desired; green or green rimmed eyes are considered a fault. Blue Persians are renowned for their

Blue-Cream Long-Hair

Blue-Cream Short-Hair

Blue Persian

flowing blue coats and enormous *ruffs*. Any shade of blue is permitted though the paler seems to be preferred. The color must be consistent down to the roots.

BOARDING: Most cats are homebodies. It is generally advisable not to take your cat with you when traveling or visiting. There are several alternatives.

Find a clean, reliable animal-boarding establishment, which might be a *pet shop,* veterinarian's, or *cattery*. Make sure cats are accepted. Check the reputation and hygiene of the place.

Sometimes you can leave a cat with friends or have a neighbor come in and feed the cat. (If so, leave detailed instructions about its care.)

The ideal solution is to find someone to stay in your house and act as a cat-sitter.

BOBCAT: a particularly American variety of Lynx found in the States and in parts of Canada and Mexico. It is sometimes also called Wild Cat, Bay Cat, and Catamount,

Jowls, ear tufts and long whiskers distinguish the bobcat.

Bobcat

and is responsible for the naming of the Catskill Mountains in New York State (*Kaatskill* means Wildcat Creek).

The Bobcat is spotted and looks somewhat like a large house cat with a bobbed tail. It is a skilled nocturnal hunter and a dextrous tree climber. Bobcats have deep purrs, high hindquarters, and white ear *tufts*.

Bobcats have been known to mate with domestic cats, and when taken young and reared in captivity, have made affectionate, interesting pets.

BONEMEAL: Made by grinding sterilized bones, bonemeal is a valuable source of calcium and phosphorus for cats, especially if they are pregnant or nursing or ill and refuse milk. A pinch may be put in the cat's food, though it is wise to check with your veterinarian first, as too much calcium can be harmful.

BONES: The cat has 230 bones, up to 25 in the tail alone (man has 206). (See also *anatomy*.)

BONES, BROKEN: Cat fractures range from mild to most serious and are most often caused by *falls* and car *accidents*. A cat with a broken bone will probably refuse to move. Keep the cat quiet, covered and warm till the veterinarian comes. If you have to take the cat to him, cover and restrain it in a towel or coat before picking up and putting in a basket. Most bones knit in ten days to three weeks.

BONES, FEEDING TO CATS: Except for heavy, flat breastbones, remove the bones from what you feed the cat. There is always the possibility of a small bone or bone splinter lodging in the throat or puncturing an internal organ. Fish and poultry bones are particularly dangerous.

BOREDOM: Symptoms of boredom in a cat are misbehavior, nipping, and lethargy. A healthy cat who sleeps all the time may be bored. The cure may be more attention or another cat to keep it company.

BRAIN: Like man, the cat has both a front brain, cerebrum, which is the seat of conscious, rational thought and a lower brain, cerebellum, which is the seat of instinct. The latter part, devoted to reflex rather than to reflection, is more highly developed in the cat.

BREEDER: a person who raises cats, often but not necessarily, a professional, whose interest is in selling and improving the line.

BREEDING: see *mating*.

BREEDING ABNORMALITIES: Abnormalities present at birth are relatively rare in the cat. Most, such as bent tails, flop ears, extra toes, crossed eyes and hidden testicles, are thought to be hereditary.

BREEDS: There are about 30 recognized breeds of domestic cat, which vary from country to country, but there are only two main classifications: long-haired and short-haired. The different breed characteristics of cats do not vary nearly as much as the different breed characteristics of dogs.

BRITAIN, CATS IN: Cats have been popular in Britain since Roman times, both as workers and as companions. The very first cat show was held in London, in 1871, at the Crystal Palace, setting a foundation for further shows and the whole idea of *cat fancy*.

The show was the brainchild of an artist and naturalist, Harrison Weir, who wanted the world to see

Judging is a complicated business that requires many experts.

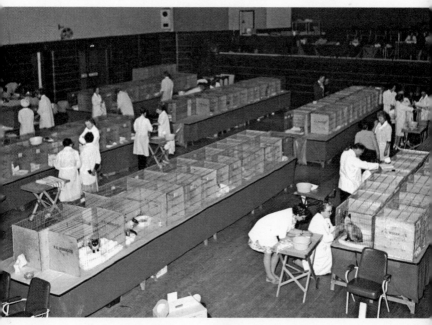

These fine specimens were top cats at the very first cat show in London.

the beauty of well-cared-for cats. It was a huge success. Since then, in the British Isles, there has been an avid interest in cats and their breeding, numerous cat shows and numerous *cat clubs*, which have been, since 1910, incorporated under one body, the

Governing Council of the Cat Fancy. This organization, made up of many affiliated clubs, sets the standards for cat shows, makes awards, and outlines the rules for registering and showing. Many outstanding champion cats have come from England, which is one of the top countries for pedigreed cats.

BRITISH: a general descriptive term often used to denote short-haired cats with round, full faces and sturdy, compact, *cobby* bodies.

BRITISH BLUE: a particularly popular British short-hair cat, a sturdy light to medium blue cat with orange or copper eyes.

BRITISH SHORT-HAIR: similar in general type to the North American *Domestic Short-Hair*, yet with a number of differences. The nose is shorter and broader, the coat is plushier, and the body tends to be stockier. They are said to descend from the first cats the Romans brought into Britain, and make excellent, affectionate pets. Varieties are Blue-eyed White, Orange-eyed White, Odd-eyed White, Black, *British Blue,* Cream, *Blue Cream, Silver,* Brown and *Red Tabby, Tortoiseshell, Calico, Spotted* and *Bi-colored.*

British Blue

BRITISH STANDARDS: the characteristics and their allotted points for the breeds recognized by the *Governing Council of the Cat Fancy*. An ideal cat with perfect characteristics would score 100. The scale of *points* is generally 50 for the type and shape, including head, ears, body, legs, paws, and tail, and 50 for eye and body color. In considering tabbies, 50 points are given for the general standard and 50 for the markings. The exact allotment varies with the breed.

BRUSH: a fancy term for the full, shortish tail of a long-haired cat.

BRUSHING: All cats need brushing. It makes their coats shiny and it keeps them from swallowing excess hair and getting hairballs.

If your cat has long hair, brush it from the tail toward the head, in short, upward strokes. Brushing in this way gets down to the roots and helps prevent tangles. In a long-haired cat, the coat should stand away from the body and the *ruff* around the face should be

Accustom a cat to brushing early in its life and it will look forward to grooming as a close, companionable time.

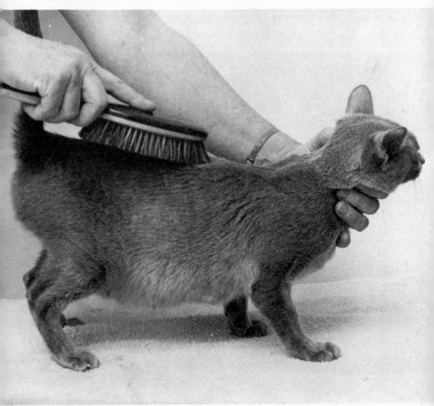

Burmese

brushed so that it forms a frame for the face. The one exception is the *tabby*. After untangling, the fur should be brushed toward the tail, the better to show off the tabby markingss

All short-haired cats should be brushed in the direction of the fur.

Most cats enjoy being brushed, and it is a good idea to establish a regular time and place to do it. Afterwards, a silk or chamois cloth rubbed on the cat's fur will make its coat shine even more.

Bristle brushes are best for long-haired cats, short rubber brushes for short-hairs. Wire brushes are not recommended.

BURMESE: an attractive breed originating in France (there called Zibelines) and introduced into the United States in 1930, by a Dr. J. Thompson. The breed was developed in the States and became recognized there six years later.

The Burmese, like the *Siamese*, is oriental looking, being long and slim and having a pointed head, large ears, and slightly slanting eyes. The main difference is in color. The most common Burmese is the Brown Burmese. An adult Brown Burmese is a uniform seal brown, with no white hairs in the coat. The shade may be slightly lighter on the chest and belly and slightly darker on the points such as ear tips, but there should be no sharp contrast. Eyes should be yellow to gold, not green.

Burmese

Though rare, there is also a Blue Burmese, which should be a rich blue-gray with slightly paler undersides.

Burmese cats are generally smaller than Siamese cats and are not quite as noisy. They are affectionate, playful, intelligent, and make excellent pets.

BURNS AND SCALDS: painful wounds caused by fire, steam, or hot water, often caused by a cat investigating a candle or jumping up on a hot stove.

If the burn is deep or covers a wide area, take the cat immediately to the veterinarian after first covering the affected area with white petroleum jelly.

A less serious burn should be treated with ice or compresses soaked in baking soda or strong tea. Afterwards, apply white petroleum jelly or a mild burn ointment recommended for cats, and lightly *bandage*. Never apply patent burn medicine without first checking with the veterinarian; in licking the wound, a cat might poison itself.

BUTTER: Smearing butter on a cat's paws and legs is a good distractive device—if you want to draw the animal's attention away from the trauma of a new house or a *bandage* elsewhere. Hopefully the cat will be too busy licking off the butter to notice anything else.

BUTTERFLY MARKINGS: tracings of this shape on the shoulders of some *tabbies*.

BUYING A CAT: see *acquiring a cat*.

C

CAGE: a wire enclosure used for carrying or shipping a cat, protecting cats from each other, and as a temporary home at cat shows and at boarding establishments. (See also *carrying case*.)

CALICO: mainly an American word used for a color combination that is also called *Tortoiseshell and White*. Calico cats may be long-haired or short-haired. The main thing is that the three colors—black, red, and cream—be clearly patched and well-distributed, and that any white be in distinct areas on the face, chest, legs, or paws. A blending of white hairs in the other color patches is undesirable. Eyes should be copper or deep orange.

Almost all Calico cats are female; the occasional male is likely to be sterile. This is one of the rare examples of a sexually linked trait in an animal, similar to such sex-linked defects in man as hemophilia and baldness.

CALLING: a term for the kind of persistent, howling cry of a female cat in *heat*, who literally hopes to summon and sexually attract a male cat.

Calico cats (tri-colored cats with white patches) are more common than true tortoiseshells, which lack the white. Only one in many thousands is a male.

Shell Cameo

CAMEO: a variation of *Persian* with *ticked* or shaded fur developed in the United States. The characteristics should be as for all long-hairs. The following are recognized:

Shell Cameo: the undercoat should be pale cream, nearly white. Tipping on the back, flanks, head, and tail should be red. However, chin, ear *tufts*, and chest should be white. Eyes for all cameo varieties should be gold or copper.

Shaded Cameo: the general look of this cat is much redder than the Shell Cameo. It may be pure red, with gradual shadings down the sides, face, and tail turning to white-cream on the chest, stomach, and under side of the tail.

Smoke Cameo: a deep red-beige cat with a contrasting white or cream undercoat apparent only as the cat moves.

Tabby Cameo: the main ground cream color should be broken by well-marked red or beige tabby markings.

CANADA, CATS IN: There is no one all-governing association; rather there are a number of progressive bodies such as the Royal Canadian Cat Club and the Canadian Cat Association, as well as afflliations with some of the American clubs. *Siamese* cats are the most popular breed; *Persians* are second.

Smoke Cameo

Shaded Cameo

59

CANADA LYNX: a member of the *Lynx* family that has gray-brown fur marked with white and lives in Canada and the northern United States. It has high hind legs, a stubby tail, broad paws, and white ear *tufts* and *whiskers*. Its favorite prey is the snow rabbit.

CANCER: Almost all known kinds of cancer are found in cats. They sometimes, however, go undiagnosed because a cat suffering from cancer may show no outward sign of pain.

Sudden loss of appetite, lethargy, failure of an ordinarily fastidious cat to keep clean, or the finding of any unusual lump or bump on or under the skin, should send you to your veterinarian.

CARACAL: an African and Middle Eastern member of the *Lynx* family that leaps so expertly it is able to catch flying birds and is such a swift runner it is able to overtake gazelles. The Caracal is a slim red-brown animal with long ears and a short tail. It is about three feet from head to tail tip.

Caracal

CAR ACCIDENTS: see *accidents*.

CARDBOARD COLLAR: a wide Elizabethan-type cardboard collar used to prevent a cat with an ear or eye disease from scratching itself and spreading any infection.

To make, take a stiff cardboard and cut off the outside corners. Then cut out an inside hole just large enough to slip over the cat's head.

CARNIVORE: any chiefly flesh-eating mammal, including cats and dogs.

CARRYING A CAT: If you have no case and have to carry a strange, sick, or lost cat, use a large thick bath towel to wrap around the cat. This both calms and comforts the cat, and protects you, as any frightened cat tends to claw. A well-wrapped cat is also less likely to escape.

CARRYING CASE: A cat carrier may be a wicker basket, a fiberboard container, or makeshift. What it is made of doesn't matter as long as it is large enough to let the cat stretch out comfortably, well-ventilated, and equipped with a clean towel or blanket, and perhaps, a favorite toy. Consideration should be given to the weather and the length of the trip. Some cat carriers have a window and some cats love to see out while others are terrified to see the world passing by. Whatever its type, the cat should be pre-acquainted with the carrier and allowed to sniff and explore it before it is put to use.

CASTRATION: see *altering*.

CAT CLUBS: associations which function in the interests of cats.

Purposes are to give cat shows, to promote projects, and simply to give people who love cats a chance to get together. Sometimes the different breeds have their own special societies.

Flexport

While cat doors are easily made at home, they can also be purchased commercially.

CAT DOOR: a flap fixed to a cat-sized hole in a door, or a special appartus with flexible, self-sealing flaps. The point is to allow the cat to come and go as it pleases (which may not be a good idea if you have an unaltered cat).

CATERWAULING: the high wailing night song of a cat, usually, but not always, stemming from sexual excitement, and always performed from a height such as a wall or roof. A caterwauling cat crouches and turns its head slightly backwards and upwards.

CAT FANCY: a special term used for those interested in the selective breeding of cats; also for any group of cat lovers.

CATS AND FURNITURE: Cats can be taught to respect furniture. Be consistent and firm about where the cat should not be. Give the cat alternatives and a catnip-scented scratching post. If you have really valuable furniture, consider *declawing*.

CATS AS WEATHER PROPHETS: It is said that a cat preening its back or the back of its ear with a wet paw is a sign of rain.

CAT HAIRS, ELIMINATION OF: Consistent, careful *grooming* helps, of course. For the most effective removal of unavoidable hairs on clothes, wind cellophane or other sticky tape around the hand, press, and pick up. (Soft bristly brushes tend merely to spread the hairs. A vacuum cleaner is effective for hair removal over a large area.)

CATNIP: Also called catmint, a member of the mint family, catnip is a plant whose dry leaves excite and delight cats. A moderate amount acts as a nerve tonic, but too much can intoxicate. Catnip also has an aphrodisiac effect on unaltered cats. It is best used for indoor cats who, in addition to enjoyment, get needed exercise playing with a catnip toy. It may also be used to attract a cat to a particular object, such as its scratching post.

CATTERY: quite literally a cat house, where cats are bred and kept, often while their owners are away. There are both indoor and outdoor catteries. Ideally there should be exercise runs and plenty of space between the cages or pens to lessen the possibility of any spread of infection.

61

A colorpoint Persian champion looking pleased and pretty as its ribbons.

CHAMPION: a *purebred* cat that has won a specified number of ribbons or challenge certificates. Championship status is mostly a matter of prestige and *stud* value.

CHARACTERISTICS: distinguishing breed traits used in tallying standard show *points*.

CHARTREUX: a French variety of cat, supposedly brought to France from Africa by the Chartreux monks. While similar to the *British Blue*, they are larger and more muscular and the coat is more gray than blue. They are gentle and intelligent and are known as excellent mousers.

CHEETAH: a large Leopard-spotted Wild Cat living in parts of Asia and Africa, which is a different genus and is, in fact, quite different from other cats. Cheetahs have certain dog-like characteristics and are sometimes trained as hunters and retrievers. They are swift runners (they reach speeds of over a mile a minute). Because they are so highly intelligent and are both trainable and tameable,

Cheetahs have sometimes been kept as exotic pets.

CHESTNUT BROWN: see *Havana Brown*.

CHINCHILLA, OR CHINCHILLA SILVER: a stunning variety of long-haired *Persian* cat. The coats should be long, flowing, and light, with silver *ticking* giving a sparkling look. (However, kittens when first born often have dark coats and shadow *tabby* markings.) The eyes should be large and expressive; green or blue-green rimmed with black or dark brown.

Cheetah mother and young.

Chinchilla

CLAWS: A cat's claws are retractable and are sheathed when not in use. Their in-and-out movement is controlled by a tendon. They are marvelously adapted for leaping, holding on, hunting, and self defense. Sharpening is instinctive.

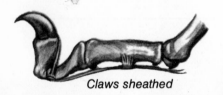

Claws sheathed

and unsheathed.

Hold claw firmly when clipping.

CLAWS, CLIPPING: An indoor cat should have its claws clipped every several weeks or when obviously needed. Hold the unsheathed claw firmly and clip only the lower white part. (The pink is the *quick* and is living tissue).

64

Use special cat clippers or blunt scissors, the former preferably. It is easiest to clip a sleeping cat.

CLOWDER: a noun that means a group or collection of cats. It is an alteration of the word "clutter."

COBBY: a descriptive word used for cats that are low on their legs, deep-chested, and rather massive across the shoulders. It denotes a squarish look. *Persian* cats are cobby; so are *Manx Cats.*

COLLARS: A collar should not be used as much for looks as to protect your cat from getting lost. It is a good idea to introduce the idea of a collar while the cat is young. Start out with a piece of colored string when the cat is still a kitten. (Be sure to check that it doesn't get too tight as the kitten grows.) An elasticized safety collar is by far the best kind, with an attached medal giving your name and address. Chains and metal collars are dangerous because they won't give if a cat accidently gets caught, and can choke a cat.

COLDS: Cats catch colds just as people do (but don't give colds to people). Symptoms are runny eyes and nose and sneezing. Keep the cat warm and out of drafts and quiet. Recovery is usually swift. If the cat is still sick after two days, consult with a veterinarian.

COLOR: The color of a cat is controlled by its genes. White is *dominant* over all other colors, while the *tabby* pattern is dominant over everything but white. Moreover, some colors are sexually linked; *tortoiseshell, calico,* and *blue-*

Two types of cat collars.

cream cats almost invariably being females.

COLORPOINT: see *Himalayan.*

COMBING: A cat should be combed to keep hairs off the furniture, *fleas* off the cat, and to keep *hairballs* from developing when the cat licks itself. It also makes the cat look nicer. Short-haired cats should be combed; *long-haired cats* must be.

The two basic kinds of combs are those with wide spaces and blunt teeth for general *grooming,* and special fine-toothed combs for getting out *fleas* and other insect pests. (See also *grooming*.)

CONSTIPATION: Some of the causes of constipation in the cat are: lack of *exercise, hairballs,* lack of liquids in the *diet,* disease, or psychic trauma such as moving to a new home. (A cat's stool

65

A cat should always be combed in the direction of the fur.

should be moist but firm; most have one movement a day but this varies.) If the constipation is mild and the cat is eating and otherwise healthy, give it raw liver, greens, half to a whole tablet of milk of magnesia, a scraping of white petroleum jelly on the roof of the mouth, or any other remedy suggested by your veterinarian. If the condition doesn't correct itself in a day or two, have the cat checked.

Constipation can be a symptom of a tumor or serious disease.

COUGAR: see *Puma*.

CROSSBREED: a cat produced by mating two *pedigreed* varieties.

CYSTIC OVARIES: a problem which causes the cat to come into season almost constantly, which is depleting to the cat and hard on its owners. Mating is likely to be ineffective. See your veterinarian.

CYSTITIS: see *bladder*.

D

DANDRUFF: the excessive flaking and shedding of dead skin cells resulting in a dull, dusty coat, and a scruffy look. Dandruff may be caused by ill health, mite infestation, or vitamin deficiency. Try giving the cat *yeast* tablets, add more fat to its *diet,* and also, rub a little olive oil into the cat's coat before *brushing*.

DDT: a poweful insecticide that is poisonous to cats. Do not let a cat into any room or area that has recently been sprayed with DDT.

DEAFNESS: Cats sometimes are temporarily deaf as the result of an ear infection. Hearing returns when the cat gets well. Cats may become permanently deaf as the result of an untreated or serious ear infection or aging. Some cats, particularly strains of blue-eyed white cats, are born deaf. (Orange-eyed whites are not congenitally deaf.)

Deaf cats can lead normal lives. They compensate for their disability by an extra sensitivity to vibrations and a fine tuning of their other senses. A deaf cat should be kept away from the street, as it is more likely to be hit by a car. (See also *ears* and *hearing*.)

DEATH OF CAT: When a beloved cat dies, there may be the problem of what to do with the remains. Unless you can give it a proper burial in the ground, call your veterinarian or local animal agency. (See also *euthanasia*.)

DECLAWING: a surgical operation done to remove a cat's *claws*, roots and all, so they never grow again. It is performed under *anesthesia,* preferably when the cat is young. Generally only the front claws are removed. It is most often done to keep an indoor cat from shredding the furniture or accidently scratching. Although some cat fanciers hotly object, there seems to be no trauma to the cat, who retains its sharpening instinct and the ability to climb. The one drawback is that a declawed cat cannot defend itself as successfully as one with claws. Declawing might well depend on where the cat lives and what kind of life it leads. (After the operation, use shredded paper rather than litter in the cat's box for several days to help prevent infection and *abrasion*.)

DEHYDRATION: a serious symptom of cat disease. To tell if a cat is dehydrated, lift the skin around

67

the neck. If it's dry and leathery and stays where you put it, the cat is dehydrated. Another symptom is gums that feel sticky to your finger. Take the cat to a veterinarian right away.

DERMITITIS: a general term for imflammation of the skin, which may be caused by allergy, insect bites, injury, age, or too much sun or sitting by the fire.

To prevent a simple condition from turning into a long-drawn-out problem, see your veterinarian for a specific diagnosis.

DEVON REX: see *Rex*.

DEWCLAW: the non-functioning inner claw of a cat's foot, which does not reach to the ground (the closest thing to the human thumb).

Dewclaws only become problems when kittens are born with double dewclaws or outsized, hanging ones, or when they grow in a circle, cutting back into the flesh. Treatment consists in cutting back the penetrating point, which is best done by a veterinarian. Old cats and cats who have been bandaged are most likely to suffer from infected dewclaws.

Dewclaw

DIABETES: if a cat drinks and eats a lot but still seems to lose weight, suspect diabetes, a disease of the pancreas. If possible, take a sample of urine to the veterinarian. Overweight, altered males are the most frequent victims. Treatment involves daily injections of insulin, which the owner usually learns to give. A diabetic cat should be treated gently because it heals more slowly than a normal cat.

DIARRHEA: a fairly common cat complaint which can be caused by a number of things. It may be the result of spoiled food, a bad *diet*, or simply of overeating—or it may be the symptom of *worms*, a tumor, or a serious illness such as *feline distemper*.

Simple diarrhea can usually be stopped by giving a mild binding medicine such as a bismuth preparation. Do not feed the cat or give it milk for 24 hours. What the stomach needs is a rest. If the diarrhea persists into the second day, call your veterinarian.

DIGITALIS: a drug from the foxglove plant used to strengthen the heartbeat of cat, as well as human, patients. It should only be administered by a professional.

DIGITIGRADE: walking on the toes, which is what gives cats their slinking gait.

DIET: see *feeding* and *nutrition*.

DINICTIS: a variety of weasel-like carnivorous ancient animal from which the domestic cat evolved. (See also *ancestors*.)

DISCIPLINE: A cat should be disciplined during, not after, a deed. Cats can be taught to respond to "No!" or "Stop!" spoken in a firm voice. Water pistols and rolled-up newspapers (banged on a table) can be used as deterrents. Never strike the cat itself. It will make it unruly and rough. It is not fair to punish a cat for what it does out of instinct.

DISEASE TRANSMISSION TO HUMANS: The diseases people can catch from cats are few and the instances are rare. *Ringworm* and *mange* are occasionally transmitted from cat to man (more often the other way around). Any cat bite or deep scratch should be promptly treated.

DISLOCATIONS: The two most common dislocations in the cat are of the jaw and the hip. There may be swelling and the cat will not be able to use the affected part.

Car accidents and falls are the usual causes. Call your veterinarian.

DISTEMPER: see *feline distemper*.

DOCKING: the cutting off of the tail. In some breeds of dogs, this is done for cosmetic reasons, but cats are only docked when the tail is irreparably injured. (The *Manx Cat* is born with a docked, or cut-off, tail.)

DOG AND CAT RELATIONSHIPS: If a puppy and kitten are raised together, they usually end up as staunch friends, playing together and sometimes even sharing food. Indeed generous cats have been known to fetch table scraps for their dog companions, while dogs have sometimes adopted kittens and protected them.

If a cat or kitten is brought into a household where there already is a dog (or vice versa), that is a different matter. The two pets

A wary meeting between a cat and dog from an early Grecian bas-relief.

A basketful of kittens—the poodle is so proud she would purr if only she knew how.

should be introduced slowly, watched carefully, and even kept apart for a few days. Some experts recommend having the cat's claws clipped so they can't cause injury in case of a spat. Others recommend letting one pet have the run of the house while the other is shut up, then switching so that the animals will be familiar with each other's scent before they actually meet.

When introduction occurs, avoid fussing and showing favorites. Let

A big dog is like a big brother to this little kitten.

them get to know each other on their own terms. Do not leave the dog and cat alone together until you are sure they are friends.

DOMESTIC SHORT-HAIR: an American and Canadian term for a cat with a short, dense coat, a well-knit body, rounded head, large eyes, and small, slightly rounded ears. The Domestic Short-Hair can be any color—red, silver, white, or black, *tabby* striped or *tortoiseshell*. In other words, it is like the majority of cats. The only difference between a Domestic Short-Hair and an alley

It's all in fun—a typical cat and dog game of tumble-tussle.

cat is that a Domestic Short-Hair is a breed, that is, cats in this category have a *pedigree*. (Some say they are descendants of the cats that came over with the Pilgrims on their voyage to the New World.)

DOMINANT: a term used in *genetics*; the one of a pair of possible traits or characteristics that most often masks the other. For example, short hair is dominant over long hair. So when a long-haired cat mates with a short-haired cat, most of the kittens will have short hair. Thus, the quality of long-hair is *recessive*; short hair is dominant.

DROOLING: When a cat purrs deeply and drools, it means it is feeling affectionate and happy. Drooling may also be a response to the sight or smell or food, a sign of fear (a cat in a carrying case may drool), or a reaction to certain drugs.

DROWNING: Grab a flailing cat by the *scruff* of the neck, because a drowning cat is likely to panic and scratch. Once rescued, hold the cat by its hind legs and let the water drain out.

Try artificial respiration if the cat is not breathing but has a heart beat. Afterwards, dry the cat. Keep it warm and quiet while you call the veterinarian. (See also *artificial respiration*.)

DRUG SENSITIVITY: Cats are sensitive patients, and as a group are more intolerant of drugs than most animals. If a cat gets sick after an injection, it may well be because of the drug used. Your veterinarian will keep track of this.

Certain comon-to-people drugs such as *aspirin* can kill a cat. Even seemingly mild skin ointments may contain ingredients that are poisonous when a cat ingests them. It is safest not to give a cat anything in your medicine cabinet without veterinary advice.

DUAL MATING: when a female cat mates with several males during a short period of time, often resulting in kittens in the same litter being sired by different fathers.

The Domestic Shorthair comes in more colors than any other breed.

EAR DISEASES: A cat's constant scratching at its ear may be a sign of ear disease, or can bring on an irritation. Cats are subject to both outer and middle ear infection; the latter may cause it to walk in a wobbly way or hold its head to one side. Foul-smelling ears, an accumulation of matter inside and swelling are signs of ear trouble. Refer the problem to your veterinarian. (See also *ear mites*.)

EAR MITES: tiny insects that look like coffee grounds and live and multiply in the cat's ear canal. The mites plus the fluid in the ear often form a nasty-smelling brown mass. Sometimes movement can be seen.

A cat infested with ear mites shakes its head a lot and tries to scratch its ears. Mites can even cause a cat to have *fits*. See a veterinarian, who will examine the cat and prescribe treatment. Ear mites can be eliminated by a combination of oil and medicine. (Carefully dispose of any swabs you use, which might contain live mites and reinfect the cat.)

EARS: A cat's ears are like small, effective sound receivers, pointed at the top and open at the base.

They contain nearly 30 muscles, more than four times as many as in the human ear. A cat's ears are also remarkable in that they turn toward the direction of sound many times more quickly than a dog's, and are receptive to frequencies of from 20 to 25,000 vibrations a second. (See also *hearing*.)

Ear cleaning should be a regular part of grooming.

EARS, CLEANING: To clean a cat's ears, use a blunt-tipped cotton swab with a little oil or petroleum jelly on the end. This should be done once a week or whenever dirt or wax accumulates.

ECZEMA: a general term for any skin disorder, often used when the exact nature of the problem is not

73

Egyptian Mau

EGYPTIAN MAU: a breed developed in the United States from cats brought over from Cairo, Egypt; recognized by some associations. The Egyptian Mau resembles the cats drawn on ancient Egyptian walls and has a similar scarab beetle-shaped mark on the forehead. In body, it is midway between the *Domestic Shorthair* and the *Oriental*. Eyes should be light green to amber and slightly slanted. The medium length silver, bronze, or patterned coat should be silky but dense, accommodating two or more bands of ticking. The ears should be large, pointed, and tufted.

yet known. Both scaly and crusty eczemas occur in cats and may be the result of heredity, *allergy,* insects, or disease. Your veterinarian can best help you identify and cure any such skin problems.

Mau-like cats are often depicted in scenes on Egyptian papyrus.

ELECTRICITY AND CATS: There is a great deal of electricity in a cat's fur; even more on a stormy day, when stroking the back may bring a shower of crackling sparks. An investigating technician said that the static electricity from one British cat caused the jumbled television images in a small town.

ELECTRIC SHOCK: Don't grab a cat that has chewed through an electric cord and is still holding on. Instead grab the cord by a thick piece of dry cloth.

Afterwards, give *artificial respiration* if needed and treat the cat for *shock*. Call the veterinarian. If your cat likes to chew on electric cords, cover them with plastic coils before there is an accident.

ELIZABETHAN COLLAR: see *cardboard collar*.

ENCOUNTER WITH STRANGE ANIMAL: In an encounter with another animal or cat, a cat is likely to arch its back and make some

European Wild Cat

sort of hissing, spitting, or growling sound. Its hair will stand on end as if the cat were saying "See how big and fearful I am. You don't want to fight me, do you!"

ENTIRE: term for an unaltered male cat with both testicles descended.

EUROPEAN WILD CAT: a completely different species and family from the domestic cat, sometimes scientifically called *Felis Silvestris*.

The European Wild Cat has a massive, muscular body, an unusually wide skull and high forehead, and a thick mackerel-patterned coat with a short, ringed, bushy and blunt-tipped tail. It may weigh up to 25 pounds.

The European Wild Cat is a highly territorial animal and a fierce predator. It has different habits from the domestic cat. It both feeds and drinks in spurts. It can quickly swallow huge quantities of meat and then not eat for several days. In winter, it is less active though it does not hibernate.

European Wild Cats cannot be tamed and rarely mate with domestic cats. There have always been a large number of them in Scotland.

EUTHANASIA: Also called mercy killing or putting to sleep, it is putting to death painlessly a living creature that is hopelessly ill or injured. The veterinarian inserts a needle containing a fatal dose of a sedative or anesthetic into the cat's vein. The animal goes to sleep quickly and permanently. Some veterinarians allow the owner to hold the cat while this is being done.

Some wild cats, such as the above, can only rarely and unreliably

EXOTIC CATS: wild cats such as *margays* and *ocelots*, which can be successfully tamed as house pets as opposed to less tameable wild cats such as tigers.

EXOTIC SHORT-HAIRS: cats comparable with *British Short-hairs*. They are *Persian* in type, and have medium-length soft fur in all the standard colors.

Cheetah

Tigrine

be tamed. They are almost never kept as pets when grown.

EYES: The cat has the biggest eyes of any animal in relation to its body weight. Its cornea is far deeper and more highly developed than that of the dog which gives it a wide and advantageous visual range.

Other interesting features are the _nictitating membrane_ (also called _haw_ or _third eyelid_) in the

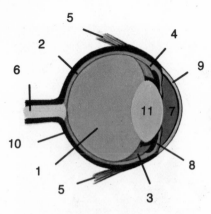

1. *Vitreous Humour* **2.** *Retina* **3.** *Ciliary Processes* **4.** *Ciliary Muscle* **5.** *Recti Muscles* **6.** *Optic Nerve* **7.** *Aqueous Humour* **8.** *Iris* **9.** *Cornea* **10.** *Choroid* **11.** *Crystalline Lens*

lower corner of a cat's eye, which helps protect the eye; the accommodating pupil of the eye, which is round in dim light and narrows to a thin slit in bright light; and the iridescent layer of cells on the retina, which reflect light and cause a cat's eyes to shine at night.

EYES, CARE OF: A cat's eyes don't normally need any special attention. If runny or irritated by the presence of a *foreign body*, bathe the eye gently with a boiled salt water solution that has been cooled (one teaspoon salt to a pint of water). Do not use old or human eye ointment. Generally, eye infections are symptoms of illness elsewhere in the body. If eye problems persist, consult with your veterinarian.

EYESIGHT: Cats on the whole have excellent eyesight, though they cannot see in total darkness. They can, however, see better in dim light than in bright light and can see ultroviolet and other rays invisible to man. They are better at seeing moving objects than at

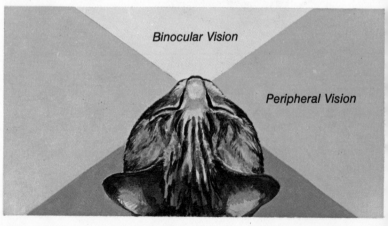

Binocular Vision

Peripheral Vision

Wide, keen, all-seeing eyes typify the cat.

distinguishing features of stationary forms such as stripes and small designs.

Experts disagree as to whether cats can distinguish colors. Some tests indicate they can; others that they can't; still others that they can only distinguish red. It may even be that the cat differentiates color in some other way than by visual sight.

The cat's field of vision is exeptional—280 degrees. (A binocular field is 130 degrees and a dog's field is approximately 83 degrees.)

FAINTING: Cats occasionally faint. Put the cat near an open window with its head lower than its body. Keep the cat quiet for a while after it has recovered.

FALLS: see *accidents*.

FATS: A cat should have some fat in its diet—for general health, a glossy coat, and to help prevent *hairballs* and bladder stones. The average cat needs about a teaspoonful a day.

FÉDÉRATION INTERNATIONAL FÉLINE D'EUROPE: an organization of Austrian, Belgian, Danish, Dutch, Finnish, German, Italian, Norwegian, Swedish, and Swiss cat societies.

FEEDING, ADULT CAT: As a general rule of thumb, a cat needs about 50 calories per pound of body weight or half an ounce of food for each pound. Thus a 12-pound cat should have approximately six ounces of food daily —at room temperature except for *milk*, which may be lukewarm. Obviously, if a cat is too fat it should be getting less; more if too skinny.

A good feeding dish is one the cat can't knock over. A second section for water is a plus. Both, of course, should be fresh.

Sunday dinner is a community affair for a family of Siamese.

Meat is the natural and basic food of the cat. An undomesticated cat prefers rodents, insects, and birds in that order. It consumes every part of its prey, thus getting muscle and organ meat and whatever vegetable matter the prey had eaten, all in all, a nutritional and balanced diet. (As an almost invariable rule, meat-eating animals eat vegetable-eating animals.)

An equal emphasis should be put on protein food for the domestic cat, whether in its natural state or in a commercial product. The diet should also be relatively high in fats, for vitamin A absorption and a glossy coat. The need for carbohydrates has not been proven, and starchy foods except in minute quantities simply aren't good for cats. The following are some of the things a cat may or should eat:

Meat: Organ meat such as kidneys and hearts are excellent. So is liver, which has a laxative effect when raw, but tends to constipate when overcooked. Muscle meat should alternate with organ meat. All cuts of beef, lamb, horsemeat, and veal are good for cats, though cats rarely like cooked ground meat. (If the meat is too lean, fat should be added.) Pork is not generally considered good for cats. There is some debate whether meat should be cooked or raw. Perhaps an indirect answer is that butcher's cats are among the most healthy. Raw meat does not make a cat vicious.

Fowl: Chicken and turkey should be thoroughly cooked, boned, and skinned, as the rubbery skin can cause intestinal trouble and cooked bones are particularly likely to splinter. Duck and goose should be fed in small portions and are too rich for daily fare.

Fish: Any kind of cooked fresh fish that isn't too oily may be given once or twice a week. It must be boned. An all-fish diet is not thought to be nutritionally sound. Canned and shell fish may also be given. Most cats find the latter a particular treat.

Baby Food: Junior beef or liver is good as an alternate, especially for convalescing or older cats.

Commercial Cat Food: varies in nutritional value. Read the label and vary the variety. Too much dry food is not good for a cat; some chewy meat or other food is needed to exercise gums and teeth.

Eggs: excellent for a glossy coat and general health. Serve mixed with other food or in milk.

Cheese: Cream and cottage cheeses are good for cats and most cats like them. Give as a meat supplement.

Milk: Well liked, but not necessary for adult cats (and it disagrees with some).

Grass and Cooked Vegetables: good in small amounts. They act as an aid to elimination.

Fruit: Give fruit in very small amounts if the cat likes it.

Oil or Butter: A teaspoon of oil or butter should be given once a day to prevent kidney and bladder trouble.

Vitamins: Use any commercial one a day type.

Any other food the cat likes: from fruit-flavored gelatin to cereal, in small amounts and as a treat.

The following are some of the things a cat should not eat: Poultry skin, bones, food that is too hot or too cold, highly seasoned food, starches, sausage rinds, uncooked pork, tea or coffee.

How many meals are given a day may be decided by the owner or by the cat. Many experts recommend one evening meal; others suggest the food be divided into a light breakfast and heavier evening meal. Most experts recommend one or two meals, though some owners give more without any obvious harmful results.

Miscellaneous notes: most table scraps aren't good for cats. A well-fed cat makes the best mouser and working cats need more food than sedentary cats. Don't leave a cat's food down more than two hours, use only clean dishes, and keep in mind that any trace of detergent smell may cause a cat to refuse its food. Some cats thrive in spite of seemingly poor or oddball diets. Some cats eat with their paws and some like to take the food out of the dish. Try to feed the cat at the same time in the same place every day. Don't bother a cat while it is eating. Finally, to a cat, the friendly spirit in which it is fed is almost as important as what it eats. (See also *vitamins*.)

FEEDING, KITTEN: Food for kittens should be warmed to room temperature. Meals should be given at well-spaced intervals and at the same time every day. Until it is three months old, a kitten's stomach is smaller than a walnut and it can't hold very much. Raw meat is fine, but no bones or highly seasoned foods should be given. Dishes should be clean, and ideally, every kitten should have its own.

When a kitten is about six weeks old, it gets its first supplementary food: kitten or baby cereal or several teaspoons of an egg yolk and milk mixture. The kitten is more likely to take the supplementary food if it is kept away from the mother for a while before eat-

A cornish Rex kitten in the middle of one of its earliest dinners.

How to get the milk without growing a milk mustache—that's the dilemma of two tabby kittens.

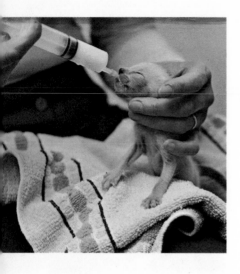

Very tiny motherless kittens can sometimes be successfully syringe fed.

ing. (Milk for kittens should be made double strength: evaporated milk or regular milk with powdered milk added, or mixed evaporated and regular milk.)

A six-week to three-month-old kitten should be fed every couple of hours, or five or six times a day. Meals should alternate between 2 tablespoons of milk-egg mixture and 1 tablespoon of minced (not ground) raw lean meat such as beef or lamb. The first meal of the

Who spilled the milk? Who cares! Let's lick it up fast before mother finds out.

day should always be the mixture. From three to four months, the number of meals should be cut down by one and cooked fish and an occasional string bean or other vegetable may be given. From four to five months the number of meals may again be reduced by one and the kitten's diet may be varied by feeding liver, heart, lungs, brains, and kidneys. At five to seven months the kitten should be eating no more than two or three times a day and the bedtime meal may be dropped. At around seven months the milk teeth are replaced by the baby teeth. The kitten is then almost a cat and should be fed like one. However you may want to keep on giving two meals for a few more months because most kittens use up a lot of energy. For added energy from three months on, a *yeast* tablet may be given several times a week. Some people swear that a *garlic* clove mashed up in the kitten's food once a week keeps the kitten worm free.

FEEDING PROBLEMS: If the cat is too fat, cut down on the amount of food you give, gradually, one half ounce at a time. If the cat is a food faddist and only likes one thing, try putting a little of something else under the favored food. If that works, gradually increase the amount of the something else. If a cat ignores his food and doesn't eat, take the dish away. Try again in a few hours. The cat may be off his feed or just feeling finicky. If it hasn't eaten a bite after 24 hours, but doesn't act sick suspect a *hairball*. If it refuses food and acts sick, call the veterinarian.

FEET, INJURED: If a cat comes home limping, take a good look at his feet. Get a light and someone to help you hold the cat.

If there is an open cut on the foot pad, clean it with warm salt water and apply an antiseptic ointment, and then bandage. Pillow the foot pad with cotton and wind the bandage well up on the leg. If nothing much shows, but the animal seems in pain, see your veterinarian. (See also *cuts* and *bandaging*.)

FELINE: belonging to or pertaining to the cat family; having catlike characteristics.

FELINE DISTEMPER: Also called feline infectious enteritis, panleikopenia and cat fever, this is the most dread cat disease. It is caused by a highly contagious virus and over fifty percent of the cats that get it die.

Young cats and kittens are most susceptible and should be protected by *innoculations* given by a veterinarian.

Symptoms are high fever, sudden loss of *appetite, vomiting,* weakness, and *dehydration*. The cat or kitten may look droopy and stand at a dish of water but not drink. It may also look hunched up, a sign of abdominal distress. Prompt veterinary attention is imperative.

Anyone nursing a cat with feline distemper at home should follow the veterinarian's instructions to the letter, stay away from other cats, and afterwards dispose of everything the sick cat touched during its illness, including bedding, feeding dishes and whatever.

FELINE INFECTIOUS ANEMIA: a virulent and often fatal cat disease caused by a *parasite*, probably carried by *fleas*, that gets into the blood stream and attacks and destroys red blood cells. Symptoms are loss of *appetite, fever,* lassitude, and pale gums. Treatment by a veterinarian includes *antibiotics* and *vitamin* therapy. The disease may reoccur and it can be transmitted from a mother cat to her kittens.

FELIS CATUS: the most commonly accepted scientific name for the domestic cat, though some zoologists prefer *felis domestica*.

FEMALE: Female cats have regular periods of *heat* and are likely to have *kittens*. If you have a female cat, and don't want kittens, it is best to have the cat spayed while relatively young (four to six months). For physical and psychic health, an unspayed cat should be allowed to mate and have kittens. Be prepared to let nature take its course. (See also *spaying*.)

FERAL CAT: a term for a domestic cat gone wild; sometimes also used for *kittens* resulting from the mating of a wild cat and a domestic cat.

FEVER: see *temperature*.

FIGHTS: Cats most often fight to protect their territory or for sexual reasons. The fiercest fights are likely to occur between unaltered males or between an *altered* male and an unaltered male. To stop a cat fight without getting scratched or clawed, douse the cats with water, throw a blanket over both, or try to get them apart with a chair.

FISH AS CAT FOOD: Fish given to a cat should be cooked and boned. It should not be too oily. An all-fish diet is not good for a cat. (Also, the cat's breath will smell fishy.)

FITS: severe upsets of the nervous system which may be caused by a variety of things: *worms, ear mites,* teething problems, *shock,* or *poisoning*.

The cat having a fit has convulsions and may twitch all over. It may screech or be silent, and it may froth at the mouth.

Do not handle a cat having a fit. Throw a heavy coat or blanket over the cat and take it to the veterinarian after it has calmed down. A fit is a far more serious symptom in an adult cat than in a kitten.

Flat-Headed Cat.

FLAT-HEADED CAT: a small (three to four pound) rare Asiatic cat with a brown coat and white underparts, widely spaced oval ears on a flatish head, and unusual facial markings—white stripes running from the corners of the eyes to the forehead, white whisker pads, and white rings under the eyes.

FLEAS: common cat *parasites* about the size of the dot over the letter i. Fleas cause itching, skin problems, and sometimes *worms* and serious disease.

If a cat scratches excessively, put it on a table and examine it carefully and thoroughly.

There are a number of good commercial flea shampoos, powders and sprays. Some experts consider powders most effective because some powder is bound to fall into the cat's bedding, and therefore, will help destroy developing fleas; others recommend sprays as being more efficient and less toxic. All recommend regular treatments for any cat, especially an outdoor cat. Use a flea comb and any good product. Do not use dog products or any with DDT. Do look for the words "non-toxic to cats." (Pyrethrum-based products are among the safest.) When a cat becomes infested, it is important to break up the life cycle of the fleas. The bedding of a flea-infested cat should be disposed of, and its surroundings kept scrupulously clean to eliminate flea eggs as well as fleas. Try to get the cat to sleep on disposable bedding such as newspapers and carefully vacuum areas where it sits.

Garlic capsules and a diet high in B *vitamins* are said to help prevent fleas.

FLEXIBILITY: The cat is remarkably flexible because it has only a trace of a collarbone and because its shoulder joints are open, enabling it to turn its front legs in any direction. Moreover, its bones are manipulated by more than 500 voluntary muscles.

FLOWERS AND CATS: Most cats love certain flowers. They smell, chew, and sometimes steal off with them. If your cat won't stay away from certain blossoms, keep them out of its reach or try another variety on the coffee table.

FLU: Also called cat flu or feline flu, it is a common disease of cats, not related to human flu. It is highly contagious and spreads fastest where there are lots of cats.

Symptoms are sneezing, crusty eyes, a runny nose, and *drooling*. There may be coughing and ulcers on the tongue. Successful treatment depends on prompt diagnosis, careful nursing according to your veterinarian's suggestions, and clean, draft-free quarters. Keep the patient well-groomed and try to keep it interested in food. Convalesence is likely to be slow, and there may be relapses.

FOREIGN: a general descriptive term having nothing to do with the country of origin referring to a type of cat that has a wedge-shaped head, almond-shaped eyes, large pricked ears, a slim body, and long tapering tail. The group includes *Abyssinians, Burmese, Havanas, Korats, Rex, Russian Blues,* and *Siamese.*

FOREIGN BODY: any unusual object that gets into the body tissue and stays there: rubber bands, needles, pins, fishbones, splinters, glass, or whatever.

Removal depends on what and where. Sometimes the object passes through the cat without harm and no treatment is necessary. In other instances (as when the cat is choking or gagging) prompt veterinary attention is essential.

Foreign White Short-Hair.

FOREIGN WHITE SHORT-HAIR: a relatively new variety of cat of a Foreign type. It should have a pure white, short, close lying coat. (Kittens sometimes have black hairs on the head which go away with a change of coat.) The head should be wedge-shaped, the ears pricked, the eyes almond-shaped, and golden yellow or bright blue in color. (See also *Foreign*.)

FOSTER MOTHER: a female cat that substitutes for the real mother in the feeding and raising of kittens. If a mother cat dies after giving birth, try to find a foster mother as soon as possible. Ask a veterinarian for references.

FRANCE, CATS IN: Cat shows have been held in France since the 1890's and cats are the most popular pets in that country. There are a number of clubs, among them the Cat Club de Paris.

The *Chartreux* is a typically French cat. The *Birman* was first established as a breed in France.

FRILL: the long fur that grows around the neck of long-haired cats, which is trained to stand up and thus frames the face.

FUR: the soft short or long-haired covering of a cat.

GAIT: the manner of movement. The cat (unlike the dog or horse) walks using both right legs, then both left legs, rather than the right front leg with the left hind leg and the left front leg with the right hind leg. Only two other animals, the giraffe and camel, walk in the same way.

GARLIC: Garlic, given mainly in capsule form, has long been claimed a remedy for *worms*. As a preventative it can't hurt, but stronger stuff and professional advice are indicated once the cat has worms.

GAS POISONING: A cat with gas poisoning gasps for breath and trembles. It should be taken into the fresh air immediately and given *artificial respiration*.

Do not leave a cat alone in a garage or room with a gas stove.

GASTRITIS: inflammation of the stomach, which may be caused by simple indigestion, bad food, or a *hairball*. Symptoms are the same as for the dread *feline distemper*—extreme thirst and *vomiting*. However, gastritis does not cause the high fever that is associated with feline distemper.

To treat simple gastritis, keep the cat off food and water for a day, though you may give it the beaten white of an egg or bismuth. (A cat hunches up when its stomach hurts; it lies on its side when its stomach is comfortable.) If the cat does not recover after a day, call the veterinarian.

GENETICS: the study of heredity. In cat breeding, the crossing of different strains produces new strains and sometimes new *breeds*. There are *dominant* and *recessive* genes. The traits of the dominant genes prevail. Therefore, *breeders* aim to establish the dominance of the most desirable traits regarding disposition and physical appearance.

The *tabby* gene is dominant over solid color, for instance, which is why more tabby than solid kittens will appear when a tabby and a solid-colored cat are mated.

Other characteristics that can be controlled by genetic selection are eye color, hair length, markings, *deafness*, taillessness, size, and certain behavior traits such as mousing ability, agility, and gentleness. (See also *breeding abnormalities*.)

GEOFFROY'S · CAT: a spotted gray or brown South American Wild Cat about three feet long, which (like the *Jaguar*) is an excellent climber.

GERIATRICS: the branch of medicine that deals with the care of the aged. (See also *aging cats and their care*.)

GERMANY, CATS IN: Much pioneering in the field of cat breeding was done in Germany. There the *Colorpoint*, with long hair and *Siamese* characteristics, was developed. Today, German purebred cats are of a high standard and are enthusiastically shown at European cat shows.

GESTATION: the period of pregnancy—in the cat, generally from 63 to 65 days, though it may extend upwards to 70 days. (See also *pregnancy*.)

GINGIVITIS: inflammation of the *gums*, which comes from improper *diet* and as a result of aging. The gums bleed and the cat is likely to lose interest in food.

Veterinary attention includes *antibiotics*, while home *nursing* may mean feeding the patient nutritious broths, rinsing its mouth, and massaging the afflicted gums.

GOLDEN CAT: a cat with a red-gold body color and striped cheeks

Golden Cat

and forehead that ranges from the eastern Himalayas to western China and is commonly called the Golden Cat of Malaya. It is thought by some to be the predecessor of the *Siamese* cat, though there is no evidence to support that belief. It is also supposed to respond to domestication and to become adept at obeying commands and learning tricks.

GOVERNING COUNCIL OF THE CAT FANCY: the British cat association under which all cat clubs are affiliated. (See also *England, cats in*.)

GRASS EATING: Most cats like to eat grass, which acts as a natural medicine and helps the cat get rid of impurities in its stomach. Occasionally though, a cat eats too much grass and vomits a grass ball. Treat as you would treat a hairball and don't feed the cat for a time.

Plant a pot of grass for an indoor cat as a special treat. (See also *hairballs*.)

GROOMING: Techniques vary but all cats need regular grooming and inspection. Most cats like to associate grooming with a special place and routine, which sometimes includes catering to individual cat whims such as putting a dab of perfume behind each ear. In any grooming session, the eyes, ears, and claws need to be checked. The former two wiped and the latter clipped if needed. The coat should be combed and brushed lightly or at length depending on its condition and on the breed. The skin should be supple, the fur shiny and free of insect pests. A well groomed cat is usu-

Regular combing and brushing is particularly important for Persian and other long-haired cats.

ally a healthy cat. (See also *brushing* and *combing*.)

GUMS: see *feline anemia, teeth, gingivitis*.

GUARD CATS: It is said that the ancient Egyptians used cats to guard their homes, temples, and warehouses of grain. They "kept away the evil eye," and deterred thieves, who thought twice before entering their domain.

Modern cats have also been known to ward off thieves by jumping on and scratching them. They have also warned their owners of fire by jumping on their beds, pawing and yowling.

HABITS: Cats like an ordered life—meals at the same time every day, their box in the same place it was yesterday, and consistent treatment.

HAIR: All cats, even so-named hairless ones, have some fuzz growing out of the hair follicles. The *whiskers* and eyebrows are special coarse hairs that also act as sensory organs.

HAIRBALLS: accumulations of hair in the cat's stomach or intestine. It is caused by the cat's licking and then swallowing loose hair. The symptoms are dry retching, *constipation*, food refusal, and *vomiting*. The best prevention is daily *combing* and *brushing*. *Long-haired cats* and molting cats are the most likely to get hairballs.

A hairball lodged in the stomach is far less serious than one lodged in the intestine. In the latter case the cat probably will refuse food. A veterinarian should be consulted right away. An X-ray should be taken and surgery may be necessary. If a hairball is suspected, but the cat hasn't refused food, it means the hairball is probably still in the stomach. Try a dose of oil, white or cat-flavored petroleum jelly, or milk of magnesia, or give the cat a portion of raw liver. Available grass and oil in the *diet* help prevent hairballs.

HAIR DRYER: an effective cat dryer as well. All cats should be dried quickly after *baths* and accidental immersions, as they catch cold easily.

HAIR STANDING ON END: A cat has a muscle under all of its skin which causes every hair to stand on end and the tail to become a bush when the cat is preening, arching, or wants to look big and threatening. (This is where the expression "wild-eyed and bushy-tailed" comes from.)

HARNESS: A harness may work better than a *collar* to lead a cat because the pull is from the shoul-

The harness should be introduced when the cat is a kitten.

ders rather than against the throat. It should be sufficiently loose and well-padded. Some cats will accept the wearing of a harness, others won't.

Havanna Brown

HAVANA BROWN: Also called Chestnut or Havana Foreign, this cat has the graceful, long, lithe, muscular body, large ears, and Oriental look of the *Siamese*, but has an all-one-color coat of warm, mahogany brown (short, but not as short as that of the Siamese). Unlike the Siamese, they have quiet voices.

There should be no Siamese markings or kinkiness in the tail. Eyes should be oval, chartreuse to green, the darker the better.

To the uninitiated, this relatively new *breed* looks similar to the *Burmese*. However, the color is darker and richer and Havana Browns have pink foot pads.

The Havana Brown makes an elegant, entertaining, and affectionate pet.

HAW: see *third eyelid*.

HEALTH: In spite of the amount of medical information in most cat books, cats in general are healthy, hardy animals requiring little veterinary attention. There is only one devastating cat disease, *feline distemper*, against which the cat may be vaccinated.

HEALTH, SIGNS OF BAD: Lethargy, a dull coat, refusal to eat, excessive thirst, *diarrhea*, and the appearance of the *third eyelid* are the most common signs of ill health in the cat.

HEARING: A cat can hear much better than a human and many experts think it can hear better than a dog. It is sensitive to frequencies up to 25,000 vibrations per second (ultrasonic noises people can't hear) and to the fine nuances of sounds. Many cat owners claim that their cats can distinguish the sounds of their owners' car motors from others on the street. Most cats also seem to like musical sounds. Of course, some cats have better hearing than others, and ninety percent of blue-eyed white cats are born deaf.

HEART: Hollow, muscular organ with four chambers, which circulates blood through the body. The blood is pumped from the veins through the heart. Carbon dioxide is released and oxygen absorbed. Then the blood is recirculated via the arteries. A cat's heart begins beating in the embryo and stops only when it dies.

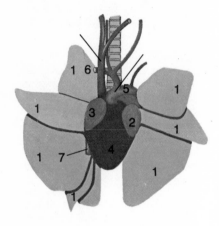

1. *Lungs* 2. *Left Auricle* 3. *Right Auricle* 4. *Heart* 5. *Aorta Superior Vena Cava* 7. *Inferior Vena Cava*

HEART DISEASE: Heart disease in the cat, compared to the dog, is extremely rare.

HEAT: Scientifically called estrus, this is the period when the female cat accepts the male. A cat may have several such receptive periods a year, but estrus is more likely in the spring and summer.

At the beginning of a heat period the cat may seem restless, rub against things a lot, and act more affectionate. Next, her sexual organs become red and hot, there is a discharge, and *calling* begins. The cat is ready to mate. The heat period stops when she becomes pregnant, or after about a week.

Cats that are not bred but are often in season may be given hormones to suppress estrus.

HEAT AND CATS: All cats love warmth and a fireplace, but some breeds seem to be able to take extremes of heat better than others. *Siamese* and *Abyssinians*

often appear to roast themselves by radiators, while *long-haired cats* may be bothered by excessive heat. Too much continuous heat can be harmful to a cat's coat, skin, and nasal passages.

HEAT PROSTRATION: affects old cats and fat cats especially. If the cat collapses after being out in the hot sun, call the veterinarian as soon as possible. Put the cat in a cool place and sponge bathe it in cold water, especially the head and feet.

Cats should not be left in hot rooms or closed cars in hot weather.

HEIGHTS: All cats are attracted to heights and sometimes they get stuck up in a tree or on a ledge. If you panic, the cat may do likewise. The best thing to do is to wait calmly for the cat to figure a way to get down.

Cats do fall from time to time though they have a better than average survival rate and tend to land on their feet.

HEMATOMA: the swelling that occurs when blood vessels burst within the tissues, forming a cyst of blood under the skin.

Cold packs will help reduce the swelling. If very large and painful, the blood bubble may require surgery.

HEMORRHAGE: profuse bleeding, which may be arterial (bright red and flows in spurts) or venous (dark red and flows steadily). It may be external or internal (in which case there may be no surface show of blood).

Symptoms of internal bleeding are pale lips and gums and weakness. To stop external bleeding until you get the cat to a veterinarian, apply a pressure bandage (gauze pads or a sanitary napkin) to the afflicted area.

Himalayan

HIMALAYAN: Also called Colorpoint, the Himalayan was produced by breeding the *Persian* with the *Siamese* to produce a striking cat with a long-haired coat and Persian body build, but with Siamese markings. The face of the Himalayan is *cobby* and the eyes are round in a Persian manner, but are a Siamese blue. Coat colors are the same as for the Siamese: sealpoint, chocolate, lilac, and red. Like the Siamese, Himalayan kittens are pale all over when born, the points appearing and darkening with maturation.

Undesirable show traits are a kinky tail, crossed eyes, and any resemblance to Siamese conformation.

HISSING: the cat's low, steam-escaping sound made when it is threatened or angry, sometimes accompanied by howling and back arching.

HISTORY, MEDICAL: You should tell the veterinarian about your cat's past medical problems, in addition to what is bothering the cat now. The more accurately you can describe the symptoms and progress of whatever is wrong, the better you can help the veterinarian come up with a quick, accurate diagnosis.

HOLDING: To hold a cat while examining or treating, put one hand on the cat's shoulders, fingers pointing frontwards. Put the other toward the rear, wherever it is most effective.

HOMING POWER: the mysterious ability of many cats to find their way to a former home, no matter how long the distance or hard the journey—even when the trip from that home was made by train or in darkness. Homing certainly involves a sense beyond the usual five but no one knows exactly what it is or how it works.

HOOKWORMS: see *worms*.

HORMONES: may be used to keep old cats active and to suppress the *heat* (or estrus) cycle.

Hormone malfunction may cause baldness, itching, and a dull or scaly coat.

HOSPITAL, CAT AT: A cat at the hospital should not be visited. A cat's *time sense* is not the same as ours and it would disturb rather than reassure it. Do tell the veterinarian in charge about any special food requirements and take his advice as to how long the cat patient should stay. A cat should

95

always be taken to the hospital in its *carrying case* and kept there while in the waiting area to keep it from getting new germs on its feet, which it might lick and ingest.

HOT: the reddish tinge in the coat of some cream-colored cats; a show fault.

HOUSEBREAKING: cats are remarkably clean animals and most often toilet train themselves to use a pan or go out into the yard.

Young kittens should be trained to a pan, however, even if there is a yard. The pan should be large, shallow, and nearby. Show the kitten the pan before it eats. Later take it to the pan and wait. Try to keep it there until it uses the pan. Afterwards, don't change the litter because you want the kitten to get the idea, which it usually does right away.

Some cats pick their own places, such as bath tubs and fireplaces. If you don't like the selection, try to barricade the area or put bags of *moth balls* around to discourage the cat.

Finally, some people train their cats to use the toilet. The best way to begin is by putting the sanitary box or tray on the toilet. Secure it well and put a slit in the bottom. Enlarge the slit as the cat gets

Newspapers under the cat pan make cleaning up easier, especially if your cat is a litter kicker.

A beloved house cat is more family than mere pet as shown in this early Victorian postcard.

used to the idea. Eventually take the tray away Some cats are more adaptable to this idea than others. A few even observe and train themselves.

HOUSE CAT: a cat kept inside as a pet, as opposed to a barn cat or a store cat kept primarily for mousing.

Most cats adapt successfully to

97

an indoors life, especially if they are surrounded by a little greenery.

HOUSEHOLD AGENTS: Be careful what you use around a cat. Strong bleaches and disinfectants used to clean dishes and sanitary pans are offensive to cats and can make them sick.

Be especially careful about sprays and insecticides. Many are poisonous to cats. Remember, particles may stay in the air a long while after spraying. Ventilate any sprayed room thoroughly before you let the cat back into it.

HOWLING: Most often cats howl for sexual reasons or as the prelude to a fight. It is a particular characteristic of unaltered males.

HUMANE ORGANIZATIONS: societies that shelter homeless animals, give medical advice and care, and often act as adoption agencies for unwanted cats and kittens. They vary in practice, aim, and efficiency. It is a good idea to investigate any you intend to use.

HUMIDITY: helps keep a cat's coat in good condition. Steam heat and a too dry atmosphere can cause excessive shedding and *dandruff*. The use of radiator pans and other such devices is helpful.

HUNTING: A hunting cat first fixes its gaze on its prey. Then it approaches in a flattened close-to-the-ground crawl. Finally, the cat draws itself up, vibrates, and then springs. The good hunter lands back paws beside its prey, teeth and claws ready to go for the victim's neck.

HYGIENE: care and cleanliness for good health and disease prevention. Proper hygiene for the cat includes regular *grooming*, ear and tooth inspection and care, good food in clean dishes, sufficient exercise, draft-free, clean bedding, and frequently changed litter in the toilet pan.

HYSTERECTOMY: see *spaying*.

IDENTIFICATION TAG: an aid in the return of a lost cat, especially important on the *collar* of an outdoor cat. Have your name and address engraved on it.

IMPOTENCE: the male cat's inability to perform the sexual act, usually resulting from vitamin deficiency or psychic upset—as when the male is taken to a strange place to be mated.

INBREEDING: breeding within the family line, for instance, brother to sister, father to daughter, mother to son.

Inbreeding purifies the strain and helps to set both bad and good characteristics. When knowledgeably done, the inbreeding of animals with the most desirable traits improves the line. (See also *genetics, outcrossing*.)

INDEPENDENCE: The cat is the only domestic animal that lives primarily and happily with people, yet has retained its independent spirit.

INDIAN DESERT CAT: a yellowish wild cat with brown ear *tufts*, black spots, and a black ringed and tipped tail. It lives in India and is about the size of the domestic cat. It can be tamed if taken young.

INDOOR CATS: Cats that live totally inside may get too much food and too little exercise. They should be given a pot of grass or some other greenery. Their resistance to disease is lower than that of outdoor cats. It is a grave mistake to think that cats that never leave the home don't need *vaccinations* or booster shots, or won't ever get *parasites* or pests. Even if the cat doesn't go out, germs and bugs can come in on people's shoes and clothing.

INFECTION: the invasion of the body by harmful bacteria or viruses, resulting in disease and illness.

INFESTATION: the invasion of the body by insects and *parasites*, which results in bodily harm.

INJECTION: the introduction of drugs into the body by a needle. The advantages are: the faster absorption of the drug, the predictability of a certain-sized dosage, and the certainty of getting the drug into difficult patients (as many cats are).

INNOCULATIONS: shots given to ward off or prevent diseases such as *feline distemper*. (For that disease, booster shots should also be given. Check with your veterinarian.)

INTELLIGENCE: It is virtually impossible to compare the intelligence of different species. Dogs learn tricks more easily than cats do, but that doesn't necessarily mean dogs are smarter. Moreover, many professional trainers have successfully trained cats. It has been shown in experiments that, next to the monkey, the cat is the quickest animal to solve a maze or figure how to lift a latch to open a door. And the cat will remember what it has learned. Rather than wear itself out with hit or miss methods, the cat often seems to think and then act. The cat's intelligence may well be more closely related to sensory perception than to reasoning as we know it. It is impossible to judge cats by human standards, but it is obvious that cats are smart, and that some cats are smarter than others. Indeed ordinary cats have done amazing things—from foiling robberies to acting as seeing eyes for blind masters to learning to ring the doorbell to get inside the house, a perfect example of how a cat tends to be clever for its own convenience.

J

JAGUAR: the only American cat among the *Panthera*. It is similar to the *Leopard*, except that rosettes on the Jaguar's coat are fewer and bigger and there are one or two black spots in the middle. The Jaguar also has a larger head, bulkier body, and the back of its ears are black.

The Jaguar is the largest American cat, a magnificent animal weighing up to 300 pounds. It is an excellent tree climber and likes swimming so much it will even go after prey in the water. A ferocious and untameable beast, it thrives equally in the mountains and jungles and on the plains. Its

Crouched close to the ground, the jaguar stalks its prey; a study in power, grace and timing.

Jaguarundi

Japanese Bobtail

habitat is the southeast of the United States and Central and South America. Its prey includes deer, small animals, birds, fish, and even alligators.

JAGUARUNDI: an unusual member of the cat family that has a weasel-like appearance and bears no resemblance to the *Jaguar*. It is a solitary animal with a long body, an otterlike tail, and a small head. Some zoologists think it should not be classified as a cat. Colors are gray and brown. The range is from Texas to Argentina. Jaguarundis have very supple bodies and travel from branch to branch as well as on the ground. They catch fish, small animals, and birds, and sometimes eat fruit.

JAPAN, CATS IN: Historically, cats there have been both worshipped and despised. The Japanese are superstitious about their cats. There are native short-tailed ones which some people prefer because they are less likely to "bewitch" humans. Sailors have long taken tri-colored or "me-kay" cats on their ships to bring good luck. The figure of a cat with its left paw raised is commonly seen in shops and sold as a souvenir. It springs from the belief that a beckoning cat brings good fortune to its owner.

JAPANESE BOBTAIL: Japanese cats that may be patched, *self-colored*, or *tortoiseshell*. They have short stumpy tails, long heads, and medium-sized bodies. They are not related to the tailless *Manx Cats*.

JAUNDICE: a yellowing of the tissues caused by bile getting into the bloodstream. It is a symptom of liver trouble and a serious condition in cats.

JEALOUSY: In spite of the fact that they are independent creatures, cats are jealous of other cats, dogs, and people. A jealous cat may try to drive away an intruder in its territory and is likely to sulk, growl, arch its back, begin washing compulsively, or attack the creature that is getting more attention than it is. That is why it isn't wise to leave an old cat alone with a new kitten or new baby until you are sure of the cat's intentions.

JUDGES AT CAT SHOWS: countries and even cat clubs have different standards and different methods of choosing judges for shows. Some show judges are appointed by committee, while others must pass certain examinations and serve an apprenticeship to an acting judge.

JUNGLE CAT: a gray-brown animal with a ringed, dark-tipped tail that lives in North Africa and Asia, but not in the jungle. Rather, it prefers the open grasslands. It is similar to the *African Wild Cat* but has more broken markings.

The Jungle Cat is larger than the domestic cat but smaller than most wild cats, weighing up to 20 pounds and being up to two and a half feet long. They are shy animals, but can be partially tamed.

JUNIOR: a show term for a cat under two years old.

Each cat at a show is judged carefully, thoroughly and impartially. Gentle hands and high standards of hygiene are musts.

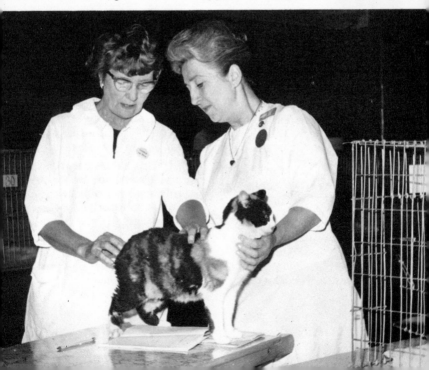

K

KHMER: a type of European *long-haired* cat with a *Siamese* coat pattern that looks similar to the *Birman*, but doesn't have the white-gloved paws. The ground color is cream, the *points* dark brown.

KIDNEY STONES: deposits of calcium that form in the *bladder* and kidney. Restlessness and an inability to pass urine may be the first symptoms. The condition is most common in male cats. Veterinary attention is needed.

KINK: a hereditary bend in the end of a cat's tail, found in *Siamese* and *Burmese*. According to current cat fashion, it may be detected by touch, but should not be obvious to the eye.

KITTEN: a young cat (for show purposes, one that is under nine months). When kittens are born, they are unable to see. Their eyes open between the eighth and the twelfth day, after which time they are highly visual and extremely curious about anything and everything. Kitten brothers and sisters are extremely sociable and friendly with each other for the first several months. Tiny kittens should be kept in quiet semi-darkness till their eyes open, in a smallish area where the temperature is even. They should be handled as little as possible during the first few weeks. Overall, kittens need much affection and mothering, frequent meals and plenty of sleep. (See also *acquiring a cat or kitten, feeding, sexing,* and *weaning*.)

KITTENING: the act of a mother cat giving birth to her kittens. The length of time may depend on the size of the litter, and the age and

Hardly a handful, a three day old blue-cream kitten.

Young kittens are naturally friendly, curious, social creatures.

previous experience of the mother, and on any medical complications.

Normally the kittens are born head first, from a half hour to an hour apart and with no complications. As each kitten emerges, the mother breaks the surrounding amniotic sac and then severs the umbilical cord with her teeth. (If the cat fails to do this the owner must help by cutting the cord with blunt sterilized scissors.) Many cats like their owners to be nearby, but some prefer to sneak off to kitten. It is important to note each *after-birth* as it appears. Consult with the veterinarian if one doesn't come.

After each kitten is born, the mother generally licks it vigorously to stimulate breathing. Do not handle the new kittens unless necessary. (See also *pregnancy*.)

KITTENING PROBLEMS: These are the most common: delayed

Most cats are careful, caring and attentive mothers.

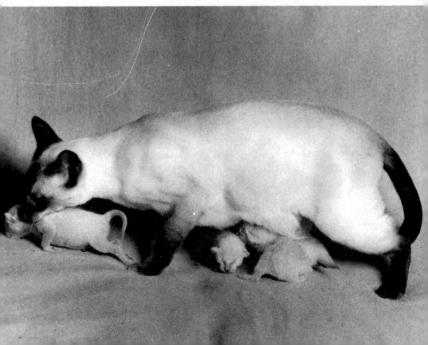

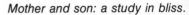
Mother and son: a study in bliss.

instinctive habit of cats formed when they are kittens. The kneading of the mother's side may make the milk flow more readily. Kneading also seems to be a sexual impulse as a mating cat may knead its partner. Overall, it expresses contentment.

KORAT: a gray-blue cat with large expressive amber eyes and a silver cast to its coat. The name means silver in Thai. A Korat is supposed to bring good luck to its owner.

The body is medium-sized and muscular, the fur is glossy and lies close to the body, and the head is almost heart-sharped. The Korat is a relatively rare cat except in Thailand, where it is highly regarded and prized. It makes a graceful, affectionate, quiet pet and an excellent companion. Korats can be trained to do tricks, such as retrieving.

Korat

birth—when no kittens have been born several hours after the onset of hard labor, consult with the veterinarian; breech birth—when a kitten is born hind first. The emerging kitten may appear to be stuck, but don't try to pull it out yourself unless advised by the veterinarian.

For some unknown reason kittens born with their eyes open usually die, and occasionally seemingly normal kittens fail and die.

KNEADING: the rhythmic lifting and pushing down of a cat's front paws against a soft object or person, accompanied by *purring*.

Kneading seems to be an

L

LACTATION: the formation, production, and secretion of milk in the mother cat, or the period of suckling which lasts for about seven weeks. The kittens begin to *wean* when they are about four or five weeks old.

Some mother cats seem to have less milk than others. If there is not enough, the owner may have to hand feed, or even better, find a cat *foster mother*. If the litter is very large or the milk supply slightly on the scanty side, begin supplementary feeding about the end of the third week.

LAMENESS: an abnormality in *gait*; limping or walking with difficulty. Carefully examine any limb that a cat puts no weight on. If you can't find any imbedded object or cut and the condition doesn't go away in a couple of hours, consult with a veterinarian. The lameness might be a sign of infection or of a fracture.

LANGUAGE: Using a variety of signs and signals, cats communicate with each other and with people. They have visual, auditory, and olfactory signals.

The olfactory signals are used mainly among themselves to define territory and to provoke sexual reactions.

The auditory signs include *hissing, howling, purring, calling,* and *caterwauling*. Cats use their voices in talking to people as well as to each other. One expert counted over 100 different distinct sounds. Moreover, each cat has its own wide variety of sounds.

The visual signals are the cat's special form of body language, produced by attitudes and movements of its ears, paws, and tail.

This cat is showing fear and apprehension.

A cat fluffs itself up to seem bigger and more fearful to an intrude

Watchful wariness combined wit
curiosity.

These movements form a kind o code.

Here are some translations o what a cat may be trying t express:

tail gently waving—pleasure

tail whipping—annoyance an warning

tail fluffed up—fear

tail held rigid out behind—abou to attack

tail held rigidly up, but with crook at the tip—a good mood

ears forward—curiosity

ears slightly back—a warning

ears flat back—about to attac

rubbing against person or thin —affectionate mood

touching with whiskers—cur iosity

widely dilated pupil—fear, pre paredness

A curious Devon Rex: note the forward ears.

arched back—a threatening pose

purring—contentment usually, pain occasionally

miaow with a rise at end—form of greeting

chirrup—Hello, here I am.

growl—anger

sharp yowl—You just stepped on my tail. (See also *purring*.)

LARYNGITIS: inflammation of the larynx which results in a low, raspy voice. The condition may be caused by infection, illness, or the constant *calling* of a cat, especially a *Siamese* or *Burmese*, for its absent owner.

Rubbing is always an indication of a good mood.

Treatment, depending on diagnosis, may include soothing syrups, *antibiotics* and tranquilizers.

CATS AND THE LAW: Cats, unlike dogs, do not have to be licensed in most communities. (Though in a number of areas, they have to be belled.) Nor are cats legally as well protected as dogs. In some states, it is permissible to collect and kill strays.

On the other hand, a pet owner is generally held responsible for a dog's actions, but not for a cat's. The feeling is that cats are roamers by nature and are more independent. Therefore, it is not your legal responsibility if your cat sees a pet canary on your neightbor's porch and carries it off.

LEAVING CAT BEHIND: see *boarding.*

LENGTH: varies enormously, though the average body length, excluding the tail is 18 inches in the female and 20 inches in the male. Approximately 10 or 12 inches should be added for the tail.

LEOPARD: a large, exceptionally beautiful yellow-gray to tawny cat with white underparts. Like the *Jaguar,* the Leopard's coat is marked with black rosettes. Unlike the Jaguar, there are no spots inside the markings. Also, the Leopard has a smaller, slimmer, more finely proportioned body. Leopards live in Africa and Asia where they prefer the wooded areas. They are excellent swim-

As seen from this old engraving and according to law in most countries, this cat is only following instinct. Its owner isn't legally responsible for the unfortunate rooster.

Leopard

mers and climbers and spend more of their time in trees than other cats. These very intelligent animals are swift, accurate killers, often going directly for the jugular vein. Unfortunately, they are now an endangered species due to the indiscriminate killing of them for their exotic coats.

LEOPARD CAT: a spotted Asiatic Wild Cat that looks somewhat like a small *Leopard*, but is from a different family. The coat color is yellow or gray, the head is streaked, and the tail is banded. Leopard Cats are also on the endangered list, having been imported as *exotic* pets.

Leopard Cat.

LEUKEMIA: a cancerous blood condition sometimes seen in cats, which is thought to be caused by a special feline virus. Since there is no cure, it is best to have the cat put to sleep.

LICE: *parasites* which live their entire lives on their animal hosts whose blood they require. There are two types, biting lice and sucking lice. Louse eggs, or nits, are attached to the individual cat hairs. Adult lice are pinhead-size, gray-blue oval bodies which can easily be seen hopping about. Lice cause a scruffy coat and weakness and tend to center around the face and joints. Treatment is by a recommended insecticidal powder. It is almost always necessary to reapply. Put newspaper under the cat you are delousing and afterwards burn the paper. Lice are less common than *fleas* in cats.

LICKING: A cat's tongue is well adapted for grooming. Cats go over their entire bodies systematically and each has its own licking routine. Mother cats also lick their newborn kittens to stimulate respiration and circulation.

LIFE INSURANCE: several companies carry animal life insurance, covering all types of cat death except those where the body cannot be found. The insured cat is identified by a nose print in the company's files.

Like Mother, like child. Licking just comes naturally.

Lion

LIFESPAN: the average lifespan of the cat is 12-14 years, but most cats (especially indoor cats) can live longer with good care. Cats have been know to live into their thirties.

The lifespan of the cat is longer than that of the dog, and difficult to compare with a human lifespan, as a year-old cat is an adult.

LIFTING: see *picking up*.

LIGER: an animal whose father is a *Tiger* and whose mother is a Lioness. Ligers cannot reproduce themselves. (See also *Tiglon*.)

LILIC POINT: see *Siamese*.

LINE BREEDING: when cats in a particular close family or line of descent are mated and remated to each other. The purpose is to keep the progeny as closely related as possible to their parents, usually in order to retain the qualities of an outstanding cat.

LION: a large, red-brown to tawny, flesh-eating member of the cat family that lives in Africa and Asia and weighs about 400 pounds.

Distinguishing characteristics of the Lion are thick hair on the mane, shoulders, head, and chest of the male, a tufted tail, spotted cubs, and a social gregariousness unusual in the cat family. Lions usually live in a group called a pride containing five or six adult cats and their cubs. Mostly, the male Lions scout the prey, which the Lionesses then kill. Lions only kill when hungry and rarely harm humans unless ill, starving, or defending young.

LIPS: the lips of a cat are black and are not used as organs of taste or touch.

LITERATURE, CATS IN: The first literary appearances of the cat were in animal fables and in bestiaries (simple moral tales with a religious base). And most often the cat was accompanied by the mouse in a chase-and-catch, stalker-and-stalked situation.

Later traits given the cat diversified. The cat was portrayed as a symbol of the mystical spirit, as a humorous, foolish or curious character, or as a creature contented and/or clever.

Cats have appeared in fairy tales, plays, poems, stories and essays. Cat authors have included Chaucer, La Fontaine, Edgar Allen Poe, Colette, Charles Perrault and T.S. Eliot. The mystic Blake created "Tiger! Tiger! burning bright," and Edward Lear, Lewis Carroll, and Don Marquis created famous, happy and nonsensical cats: the seafaring cat in the *Owl and the Pussy Cat*, the Cheshire Cat in *Alice in Wonderland* and marvelous Mehitabel in *archie and mehitabel*.

In fairy tales, the most famous cat is Perault's *Puss in Boots*,

This English illuminated Latin folio was written in the 12th Century.

114

The essence of the beauty and mystery of all cats is caught in William Blake's classic poem: The Tiger.

The imaginative Cheshire Cat in Alice in Wonderland.

Alice awakes after her dream, back home with a clutch of kittens.

A Beatrix Potter drawing in The Sly Old Cat, *combining a marvelous sense of form and feeling for children.*

Cats are found in every kind of humor.

here was a Young Person of Smyrna, whose grandmother threatened to burn her;
  But she seized on the cat, and said, " Granny, burn that!
      You incongruous old woman of Smyrna ! "

PANTOMIME

Two very different kinds of cat in two very different British versions of Puss in Boots.

Dick Whittington's cat was supposed to have been a matigot, a magical
and good fortune-bringing black cat.

The Pussy Cat seems to be getting the better of the Owl in this rendering.

LITTER BOX: Also called sanitary pan, a litter box is any plastic, cardboard, or metal tray, pan, or box filled with shavings, paper shreds, sand, or commercial litter that is used as a cat's indoor toilet.

Disposable litter boxes are most often used for sick cats, in *catteries,* and when traveling with a cat. Otherwise, the best tray is one that is sufficiently large and can be thoroughly cleaned. (See also *housebreaking*.)

LONG HAIR: The exact origin of long-haired cats is not known. While it is true that wild cats living in cold climates have long fur, most authorities think this has no bearing on the domestic cat. The general opinion is that long hair developed as a mutation in short-haired cats, and that the characteristic became established over a period of time.

LONG-HAIRED CATS: a term often used synonymously for *Persian*.

LONG-HAIRED COLORPOINT. the Himalayan breed as it is known in England. (See also *Himalayan*.)

LOUD NOISES: Cats hate loud noises and may panic, especially when the noise is sudden and unexpected.

LYNX: any of several wild cats of the genus *Lynx*, including the *Bobcat, Canada Lynx,* and *Caracal*. All have long legs, short, bobbed tails, and tufted ears.

Lynx

M

MACKEREL-STRIPED TABBY SHORT-HAIR: Some call this cat the true striped tabby and the original domestic cat. The stripes should be narrow and distinct from the background color. The rings should run vertically from the spine to the ground and be plentiful.

MAINE COON CAT: Also called Maine Cat or Coon Cat, this is a big, solid-looking, long-furred cat whose origins are open to speculation. One story tells that the Maine Coon Cats are all descendants of the cats brought over by a Captain Coon in the early days of American history. Another (impossible) suggestion is that these cats were the result of matings between domestic cats and raccoons in early New England. The most likely explanation is that the original cats, Angora-types, were brought to the New World by sailors, and after mating with some of the domestic cats and becoming hardier by natural selection due to the long, cold winters, emerged as the type known today. They are sturdy cats with broad faces and long fur, but with less undercoat than other *long-haired cats*. Also, unlike other long-haired cats, the tail ends in a point rather than a bush.

Maine Coon Cat

Maine Coon Cats are not an officially recognized *breed* but they have their own special shows and admirers. They make lively, intelligent pets, and are unsurpassed mousers. These striking looking cats come in all colors and color combinations, though tabby predominates.

MALTESE: a name sometimes given to any American short-haired cat similar in type to the *British Blue*. Colloquially, any blue cat may be called Maltese.

MANGE: a skin disease caused by microscopic mites. Symptoms are crustiness, sores, itchiness, and bald patches. Suspect mange if there are such patches around the face or feet. However, because there are two kinds of mange and the disease resembles others, it is best to consult a veterinarian. Treatment is somewhat long and drawn-out and is usually carried out at home because mange is highly contagious.

MANNER OF MOVING: Cat are among the most graceful animals in the world. They have several *gaits* and are one of the few animals to walk using both right feet, then both left feet. They leap with spring, climb with agility, and stalk with precision and power.

MANX CAT: a solid compact cat without a tail, as a result of natural mutation. The Manx Cat also has unusually long hind legs and a high round rump, which gives it a somewhat hopping gait and leads to its nickname, "rabbit cat."

Manx Cats do not necessarily breed true as two *purebred* Manx Cats may produce kittens with

A Blue Cream Burmese walking at a stealthy pace.

Margay Cat

Manx Cat

stumps of tails. (Ideally, for show purposes, there should be a hollow where the tail would normally start.)

Manx Cats are swift runners and good mousers, and have an excellent sense of balance in spite of their lack of tails. They make bright, affectionate pets, and have unusual soft voices.

Their coats may be of any color or pattern. Eye color varies from yellow to orange to green (or even blue for a white cat). The coat itself is double: a dense undercoat and an open, soft top coat.

Manx Cats are said to have come from the Isle of Man. Some trace them back as far as Noah's Ark. The legends about Manx Cats are many and varied.

MARGAY CAT: Similar and related to the *Ocelot*, the Margay is a small wild North and South

American cat. It is Leopard-spotted, has huge, expressive eyes, and weighs up to sixty pounds. It is nocturnal and carnivorous, a fearless fighter yet adaptable and relatively easily tamed and trained. Margays have made excellent pets though they are by no means as predictable or as easy to live with as their domestic cousins. Successful taming depends on a Margay's being acquired from a reliable source while young.

MARKINGS: Wild and domestic cats come in several basic patterns: self (all one color), patched, tabby-striped, spotted, tiger-striped, and oceloid.

MARMALADE: a word used to describe a non-pedigreed ginger or orangish-colored cat, usually with *tabby* markings. Marmalade cats are almost always male. They make sturdy, good-natured pets. (See also *Red Tabby*.)

MASK: dark face coloring as on a *Siamese* cat.

MATAGOTS: magician-cats that have power to bring wealth to a home where they are well-fed. According to French legend, a matagot, or magician-cat, must be lured by a plump chicken, then put into a sack and carried home without its prospective owner once looking backwards. There, at each meal, the matagot must be given the first mouthful of food. In return it will give its owner a golden coin every morning.

In England, Dick Whittington's cat was a matagot who brought its owner good fortune and changed his luck from bad to good.

MATING, DUAL: When the female cat is impregnated by more than one male cat, she may produce young that have different fathers or even litters in which every kitten has a different father. This happens because the female produces a number of eggs; if she mates in succession, one egg may be fertilized by the first male, another by the second and so on.

Some experts think most natural matings are dual, as opposed to organized matings of *purebred* cats. Incidently, it is impossible to determine which father sired which kitten.

MATING, NATURAL: Cats are naturally, and sometimes passionately, interested in the opposite sex and occasionally in substitute displays of affection directed towards people and animals of other species.

The female cat in *heat,* or season, begins to rub and purr. As she get more excited, she may call, paw the ground, or roll over. *Siamese* females are especially vocal.

If she has the opportunity she will soon call and be surrounded by *tomcats* fighting for her favors. She may mate with just the winning cat, a cat on the sidelines while the winner is being decided, or a number of males in succession, which may be nature's way of making sure the female gets pregnant.

Cats under the same roof tend to be more monogamous. Sometimes the male will pursue the female, courting her for several days without food before obtaining and mating her.

During the sexual act the female crouches in front of the male, who

Not all father cats are aloof. Some, depending on disposition and domesticity, take to the role of faithful husband and protective family man.

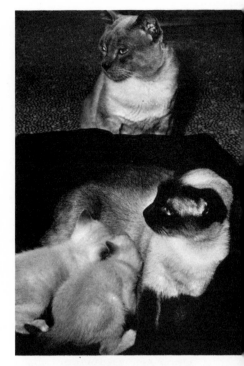

mounts her and grabs hold of the *scruff* of her neck with his teeth. The male cat then kneads the female's sides and moves his pelvis in rapid thrusts until ejaculation occurs.

Afterwards, as the male withdraws, the female utters a loud cry. Some think this is a cry of ecstasy because the female is usually ready and willing to mate soon again. Others think it is a cry of pain because the penis of the male cat is barbed. (Scratching of the vagina may also be the nervous stimulation that begins ovulation.)

The period when mating can occur usually lasts four to seven days. (See also *dual mating*.)

MATING, STUD: Cats seem to mate less easily in the artificial atmosphere of a *cattery* or stud house. However breeders mate cats in such places because they do not want a valuable cat mauled or hurt in a cat fight over a female. In stud mating there is just one male for one female.

It is general practice that at least one of the cats be experienced and that the cats be in adjacent cages and introduced before mating. There is some debate, however, about the number of times the female cat is mated. Some breeders say one mating is sufficient; others allow a second just in case the first is unsuccessful.

Cats being artificially mated are likely to be more nervous than cats in natural surroundings. The female may try to claw the male,

or the male, away from familiar surroundings, may be impotent.

MATS AND TANGLES: snarls and clumpy lumps of tangled hair to which *long-haired cats* are prone. Sometimes a mat can be teased apart with a knitting needle or other bluntish instrument. (Wetting the hair first often helps.)

If you have to cut a mat out with scissors, cut with the hair and point the scissors outwards.

If a *Persian cat* strays and comes home one mass of mats or gets in the tar pot, it is best to take the cat to the veterinarian.

MEALS FOR GROWN CATS: Opinion varies between giving one main (usually evening) meal and two meals a day (breakfast and dinner). Usually the cat will estab-

127

The veterinarian using a plastic syringe to give a cat its medicine

never certain how much medicine has actually gone down.

The best way to give a pill is to force the cat's mouth open with the fingers of one hand while you put the pill as deeply back in the throat as possible. Then hold the mouth closed and massage the throat gently. Butter will make the capsule slide down more easily. Putting a few drops of water on the cat's tongue before you give the pill or rolling the pill in meat or something solid the cat likes are other ploys.

The best way to give liquid medicine is to use a plastic medicine dropper. Measure the dose, force the cat's jaw open, and aim far back towards the base of the tongue. Do not tilt the head back or the cat can choke. Some cats prefer being spoon-fed. Others are so skittish that the only way to get the medicine down may be to smear the cat's forelegs with it, so that the cat then licks it off.

If nothing seems to work, ask your veterinarian for suggestions and perhaps a demonstration.

Some general guidelines on medicine giving: don't give the cat dog medicines, don't give anything externally that will harm the cat if it licks it off and ingests it, and try to remain calm and purposeful yourself. Cats inwardly sense nervousness and indecision and react adversely to it.

lish its own pattern. (See also *feeding*.)

MEDICAL SUPPLIES: Some recommended items for a cat's medicine chest are:

    rectal animal thermometer
    sterile cotton pads
    bandages
    plastic medicine dropper
    non-carbolated petroleum jelly
    oil (olive or baby)
    flea spray or powder
    carsickness remedy
    milk of magnesia
    mild antiseptic or peroxide
      solution
    tannic-based ointment for burns
    diarrhea remedy

MEDICINE, GIVING: Some experts suggest mixing medicine in with a cat's food. It may work, but there are two major problems: the cat may then refuse both the food and the medicine, and it is

MELANISM: black *mutation*, the opposite of albinism. An example is the black *Leopard*, commonly called a *Panther*.

MEMORY: There is a lot of talk, but not much scientific proof, about how well a cat can remember. Most cat owners can tell stories about cats seeming to recognize familiar lost toys and favorite places. Memory may be a part of the well-known homing instinct of some cats, who travel miles to return to an old home even after a year or more has past.

MEXICAN HAIRLESS CAT: virtually hairless cats with pointed heads, big ears, and long whip-like tails that were produced by *mutation* and looked like a cross between a cat and a rat. Supposedly, there were two of these mutations, a brother and a sister.

Mexican Hairless Cat.

The brother was killed by a dog before the breed could be established.

Other hairless and almost hairless kittens have appeared from time to time, but no one has ever been able to breed them successfully.

MILK: necessary for kittens but not a must for adult cats. Some cats like it; some don't; others are allergic to it and in others it may cause *diarrhea*. Even a *nursing* cat's calcium needs can be met by other foods—cottage cheese, bone meal, and vitamin-mineral supplements. Never leave milk stand more than two hours, and never feed a cat an all-milk diet.

MOLT: the normal yearly shedding of a cat's hair, usually in the spring or autumn. Kittens molt when one year old regardless of the season.

MONGRELS: cats of uncertain parentage whose *pedigrees* cannot be traced—in other words, most cats. Unlike mongrel dogs, however, mongrel cats have the same basic shape and a similar look. This is primarily because generations of cats have not been so selectively bred to favor certain characteristics. There is far less basic difference between a *Persian* and a *Siamese* than between a Newfoundland and a Chihuahua.

MOTH BALLS: a useful device to keep cats off delicate chairs, rare silk rugs and dangerous ledges. The strong odor will repel the cat and discourage it from the area.

MOTION SICKNESS: *vomiting* and other temporary signs of illness caused especially by car travel. Don't feed a cat prone to

A cat contemplating a field mouse, and its next move.

motion sickness for at least six hours before starting out. Three quarters of an hour before leaving, give the cat a half tablet of a car-sickness remedy. Repeat the dosage after two hours if the cat seems to need it.

MOUNTAIN LION: see *Puma*.

MOUSERS: cats that chase and catch rodents and are helpful in eliminating those pests on farms, in granaries, and around stores. Some cats are better mousers than others. *Maine Coon Cats* are supposedly excellent mousers while *Manx Cats* are particularly adept in spite of their lack of tail.

Many domestic cats hunt for sport rather than food. However, an all-mice diet is not adequate for a cat. Supplementary food should be offered and a good mouser is invariably a well-fed, healthy animal. Also rat catching can be a dangerous sport, as many rats carry disease and rat bites very often become abscessed necessitating veterinary attention.

MOVING TO A NEW HOME: After moving, contain the cat in a closed room with some of its familiar belongings (a bathroom is less likely to have the movers traipsing in and out). When things have set-

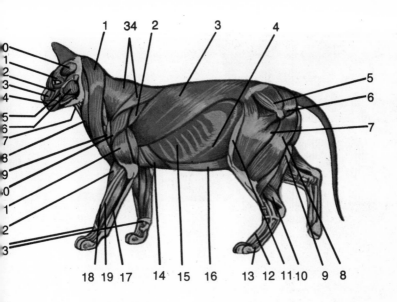

Muscles 1. *Cephalo-humeral* **2.** *Infraspinatus* **3.** *Latissimus Dorsi* **4.** *Great Oblique* **5.** *Gluteus Medius* **6.** *Gluteus Maximus* **7.** *Fascia Lata* **8.** *Biceps Femoralis* **9.** *Semi-tendinosus* **10.** *Gastrocnemius* **11.** *Sartorius* **12.** *Extensor Tendons of Toes* **13.** *Flexor Tendons of Sole of Foot* **14.** *Pectoralis Major* **15.** *Serratus Magnus* **16.** *Rectus Abdominis* **17.** *Flexor Carpi Ulnaris* **18.** *Flexor Carpi Radialis* **19.** *Extensor Communis Digitorum* **20.** *Temporalis* **21.** *Orbicularis* **22.** *Nasalis* **23.** *Maxillaris* **24.** *Zigomaticus Labialis* **25.** *Zigomaticus* **26.** *Masseter Muscle* **27.** *Sterno-hyoid* **28.** *Mastoideus* **29.** *Acromion Deltoid* **30.** *Scapula Deltoid* **31.** *Triceps* **32.** *Extensor Carpi Radialis* **33.** *Anular or Wrist Ligament* **34.** *Trapezius.*

---

ed, let the cat sniff and explore he new house. Then feed the cat. If the cat seems particularly nervous, smear *butter* on its paws to preoccupy it.

MUSCLES: the movement-producing tissues that hold the *skeleton* together. The cat has over 500 voluntary muscles as well as numerous involuntary ones. Unlike most other animals it can raise the hair on its back by mus-

cular activity and move in a rotary motion as well as backwards and forwards.

MUSIC, CATS IN: A composition by Scarlatti known as the "Cat's Fugue" is thought to have been suggested by a cat's walking across the keys of a harpsicord. Ravel wrote an opera about cats based on a short story by Colette. **MUTATION:** in *genetics,* the sudden departure from parent type

Cats themselves have a wide and varied vocal range. Perhaps that is one reason they are considered music lovers.

caused by a change in a gene or chromosome (resulting in offspring different from parents in hereditary characteristics). Mutation, with carefully controlled subsequent breeding, may lead to the establishment of a new *breed*.

MUZZLE: the projecting part of the head of a cat, including mouth, nose, and jaw.

N

NAILS: see *claws*.

NAMES: Most cats learn to recognize their names, though they will not necessarily respond when called.

The name itself may be anything you find imaginative and appropriate. When scolding, use a firm "No!" rather than the cat's name to avoid the cat's associating its name with being punished.

NERVOUSNESS: Cats vary greatly in temperament. Some are more jumpy and skittish than others. Excessive nervousness in cats may be caused by poor breeding or a nervous owner. Kittens unused to people are inclined to make nervous adult cats. Some cats never get over their nervousness, but others are greatly helped by patient, affectionate handling, and occasionally, tranquilizing drugs obtained from a veterinarian.

All cats are made nervous by sudden loud noises and jerky movements as they have finely tuned, swift responses. Also, a cat's tentative looking about, pawing and poking in a new situation is cat nature rather than a case of nerves.

NETHERLANDS, CATS IN: Dutchbred *champion* cats are seen in all European shows, and there are a number of important *cat clubs* in that country.

NEUTER: to sexually *alter* a cat, that is, to *castrate* a male cat or to *spay* a female.

NEW ZEALAND, CATS IN: There is a large cat following in New Zealand and many cat shows are held, some of them in connection with agricultural shows. The controlling body is called the New Zealand Governing Council of the Cat Fancy.

NICTITATING MEMBRANE: another name for the *third eyelid*, that begins at the inner corner of a cat's eye and helps keep the eye free of dust.

In New Zealand, the Blue-cream Long Hair is a particularly popular breed.

The colder it gets, the better the Northern Lynx likes it.

NORTHERN LYNX: a beautiful, faintly spotted yellow to cream Wild Cat with silvery guard hairs, giving it a most exotic look. The ears are long and tufted; the tail tip black. Northern Lynxes are still found mainly in the Northern Hemisphere, particularly Alaska.

NOSE: the external part of the smelling apparatus, which is small and broad and extremely sensitive in the cat. A healthy cat's nose should be cool and slightly moist. If dry, the cat's sense of smell is impaired. When a cat runs its *tongue* over its nose, it is a sign that it doubts the worth of its food.

NOSEBLEEDS: Nosebleeds are fairly rare in cats and most of the human remedies such as ice packs and elevating the head make the cat panic. If the bleeding is moderate, the best thing to do is leave the cat alone in a quiet place. Hopefully a clot will form. If the bleeding is severe, call a veterinarian. Most common causes

134

Rx: tender loving care for the sick cat.

are *falls, foreign bodies,* and respiratory troubles.

NURSING: Following are some general pointers on the home nursing of a sick cat:

Handle the cat as little as possible. Do what you have to but don't fuss over the patient.

Keep the cat warm.

Keep it out of drafts. Pad the bed with newspaper and blankets.

Keep the cat in a confined place. A feverish cat may wander into a cold room and become more ill.

Provide fresh water and change it frequently.

A convalescent cat needs rest and quiet, preferably in a contained environment.

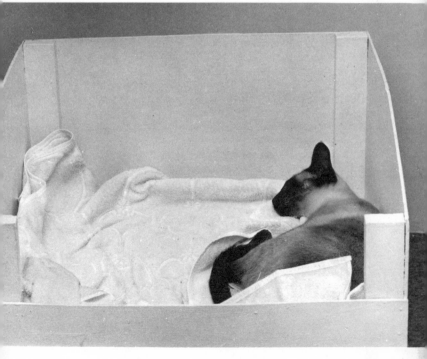

It is thought that the kneading of the kittens against the mother's side helps stimulate the flow of milk.

Change any soiled bedding.

Groom the cat to help it keep its self-respect. Wipe eyes free of matter and gently comb and brush its fur.

Dim the lighting to encourage rest.

Ask your veterinarian about special *diet* requirements. (Meat pieces plus broth may be liquified in a blender for cats with tooth or throat troubles.)

Give the prescribed drugs at the proper times, but don't give unrecommended medicines from your own medicine chest.

NURSING CAT, FEEDING: Feed a nursing mother cat what she would normally eat, with the possible exception of adding more *milk* and calcium-related products to the diet. Divide the food into more frequent meals of slightly smaller proportions. Be sure the cat has plenty of water. Ask your veterinarian whether you should give a *vitamin-mineral* supplement.

NURSING KITTEN, FORMULA FOR: It is difficult to substitute other milk for cat's milk if you have to nurse kittens yourself. There are commercial preparations, or dog's milk may be used as it is closer to cat's milk than cow's milk. Consult with your veterinarian. Remember to sterilize the bottles before each use. (A doll's bottle is close to the right size; sometimes the tip of a sterile handkerchief squeezed in the milk is the only thing that works.)

NUTRITION: the study of foods: what sustains, what promotes growth, what helps the body repair itself, and what provides energy. For good nutrition, no one food should be eaten exclusively. The emphasis should be on protein (meat and fish), which cats utilize with the utmost efficiency. Cats also need fats, which they digest well, minerals such as potassium, calcium, iodine, sodium, and vitamins, particularly A, D, E, and the B complex group. The need for carbohydrates is debatable. Cats certainly do not need them in the degree humans do.

Deficiency diseases occur when a cat or kitten severely lacks one of the necessary elements of nutrition. Protein deficiency may result in weight loss and limb swelling; calcium deficiency in brittle bones (especially in kittens that don't drink enough milk); iodine deficiency in kittening problems; vitamin A deficiency in poor coat and vision; vitamin D deficiency in bowed legs; and vitamin B deficiency in anemia, kidney disease, and loss of appetite (most often the result of an all-canned food diet). The whole subject is vastly complicated and even the same basic foods vary in nutritional value according to how they are prepared and preserved. If you suspect a deficiency disease, consult with your veterinarian. Carefully read the labels on canned foods. (See also *feeding* and *vitamins*.)

"It doesn't look like mother but it fills my stomach." An orphaned Siamese kitten eagerly accepts a bottle substitute.

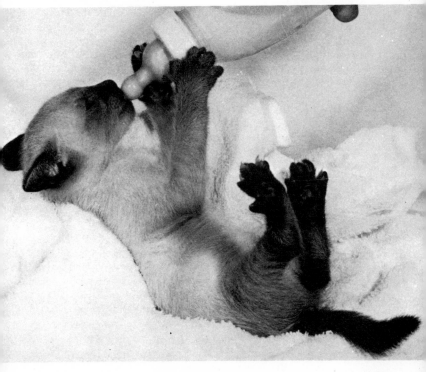

O

OBESITY: Too much extra fat isn't good for any animal. An obese cat should probably have more exercise and less food. A sedentary indoor cat needs considerably less food than its outdoor cousin. (See also *overfeeding*.)

OCELOT: a beautifully marked spotted Leopard-like cat which is in danger of becoming extinct because its fur has such great commercial value.

Ocelots range from the southern United States through South America. The background coat color is gray-yellow or brown-yellow covered with dramatic black spots and dark lines on the face, running from the nose to the forehead. The tail is ringed and the underparts are of a lighter color. The Ocelot is about four feet long including the tail. Females are slightly smaller, but males weigh about 35 pounds. This beautiful wild cat is a good climber and swimmer, and a skillful hunter.

Ocelots tamed as kittens have made *exotic* and affectionate pets. However, they are not totally reliable, especially around chickens and small dogs.

OCICAT: a cat developed in the United States, the result of a cross-mating between a chocolate-point *Siamese* and a crossbred *Abyssinian*-Siamese. The variety has short silky cream-colored fur with chestnut- or chocolate-colored spots, golden eyes, and *tabby* markings on the throat, legs and tail.

OIL: Cod liver, olive, and other vegetable oils are sometimes used 1) as a dietary supplement to add *vitamins* and make the cat's coat shinier, 2) to promote regularity, and 3) as a mild cleansing agent for eyes and ears.

OLD AGE, SIGNS OF: in the cat these include white hairs around the muzzle, a seeming fear of leaping, more sleeping, *constipation* and kidney trouble, *deafness,* and tooth decay.

OLD AGE, TREATMENT OF IN CATS: An older cat needs more affection and sleep. Exercise is

Ocelot

138

This Egyptian bronze cat dates back to around 2400 B.C.

also needed though string chasing may substitute for mouse chasing.

An older cat may need softer foods and a *vitamin-mineral* supplement. Warmth is also important as the older cat is more likely to catch cold.

Any cat over eight or nine years old should have a yearly check-up by a veterinarian, as well as home checks of *teeth* and *paws*.

ORIENTAL: descriptive of the slanted eyes of *Siamese* and other similar *short-haired cats*.

ORIGIN OF THE DOMESTIC CAT: The domestic cat as we know it is supposed to have originated in Egypt, but nobody seems to know quite how or when. The cat was not domesticated as early as the dog, though there is a picture of a cat with a collar around its neck in an Egyptian tomb of the fifth dynasty (about 2600 BC). Of all the current domestic breeds, the *Abyssinian* is closest to the original Egyptian cat.

The early Egyptians worshipped the cat and called it Mau, which sounds like miaow. Killing a cat was a crime punishable by death, and a man was supposed to shave his eyebrows as a sign of mourning when his cat died. The exportation of cats was forbidden for, thanks to the cat, the Egyptians could raise their crops and store their grain without fear of its being destroyed or their being overrun by rats, the classic Egyptian plague. There seems to be no evidence that either the Assyrians or the Hebrews kept cats as early as the Egyptians. Neither did the Greeks, who later stole cats from the Egyptians to preserve their own harvests. Cats are pictured in wall tiles dating from the First Minoan period (1600 BC).

In the European area, the cat went from Portugal to Scotland, where wild cats still abound. It is said they came indirectly from an Egyptian army commander who survived the mass drowning of the Egyptian army in the Red Sea after Moses parted and then reclosed the waters and led the children of Israel to freedom. According to the story, the army officer escaped to Portugal with his wife, the Pharaoh's daughter, and her cats.

139

An eighteenth century engraving shows various breeds of cat in relative sizes from the Lion to the Domestic cat.

To the early Scots, the cat was a mighty warrior as well as a guardian of grain. Fighting cats are common on highland crests and mottoes, and the word cat was also used for a fighting man. Cats spread in the European area and were generally favored until the Inquisition.

In America, the first record of the introduction of a domestic cat is in the chronicle of a French missionary who, as a token of friendship, gave a cat to the Huron Indians. The Indians accepted the cat but left it to die, not realizing its value as a rodent killer. In 1749, cats were imported into the New

This engraving shows Chinese cat merchants plying their trade.

World when colonies in Pennsylvania were overrun by a plague of rats. The popularity of cats in the States has spread up to today, when there are an estimated 40 million cats.

ORPHANS: kittens that have lost their mother. If possible, find a cat *foster mother*. (Before introducing, smear the kittens with some of her milk so the orphans won't smell strange to her—she will be less likely to reject feeding them.)

OUNCE: see *Snow Leopard*.

OUTCROSSING: the breeding of cats from different blood lines or strains within the same *breed*. After successive inbreeding (which tends to produce smaller animals), an outcross is often done to preserve the vigor of the line. (See also *genetics, inbreeding*.)

OVERFEEDING: Overfed cats usually get too many and too large meals. Cut down on the portions and the number of meals. Don't give the cat tidbits from the table when it is not its mealtime. It isn't good for a cat to be fat. (See also *obesity*.)

OVULATION: the discharge of eggs from the cat's ovary, which always comes after, and is a result of, copulation.

OXYGEN: given in veterinarian practice to cats in *shock*, as an aid to *anesthesia*, and sometimes in *pneumonia* cases.

P

PADS: the soft cushioned underparts of a cat's foot. Pads enable the cat to walk on rough, irregular surfaces without injury. There is one pad under each toe and a larger one behind the toes, similar to the human heel. If a cat is limping, look for a foreign object imbedded in a foot pad. Soothe cracked pads with cod liver or olive oil. Put a special stocking bandage on a cut pad.

Underside of Fore Paw. *1 2 3 4: front pads; 5: dew claw; 6: carpal pad; 7: "heel" pad.* **Underside of Rear Paw.** *1 2 3 4: front pads; 5: "heel" pad.*

PAIN: A cat in pain may become restless or be lethargic, may *purr* in a different way or be totally silent. It may try to favor an injured part or hold it stiffly. It is impossible to accurately estimate degrees of pain in cats. However, they are such highly developed animals that they undoubtedly feel it keenly.

Pallas' Cat

PALLAS' CAT: a wild cat with a singularly low forehead, stripes slanting down the face, and a bushy ringed tail. The Pallas' Cat inhabits the rugged rock country from the Caspian Sea east to Tibet and Mongolia. The coat is long and either a silver-gray or orangish. Two unusual features are white and black rings around the eyes and widely spaced ears, which have caused some experts to speculate that the Pallas' Cat hunts more by sight than by sound.

An old print of a Pampas Cat in its preferred grassland habitat. It is now a nearly endangered species.

PAMPAS CAT: a silver-gray Wild Cat with reddish stripes found in Peru and Brazil, which weighs about 30 pounds and is said to be untamable.

PANTHER: a black Leopard.

PANTING: not a sign of danger unless a cat is old or has a bad heart.

Pampas Cat

143

PARALYSIS: unlikely in the cat and sometimes only temporary, but always a matter for prompt attention by a veterinarian.

PARASITE: A parasite is a plant or animal which depends on another plant or animal for its life and lives at an unwilling host's expense, as a *tapeworm* in a cat's intestines or *lice* that suck its blood.

Getting rid of parasites permanently means doing them in at the weakest link in the life cycle, whether as eggs, larvae, or adults. Frequent cleansing of the cat's surroundings is imperative.

PAWS: the feet of an animal with *claws*. Cats use their paws to attract attention, show affection, feel textures, play, and push objects, as well as to walk upon and to wash themselves. In the wild, a cat may instinctively wash its paws to remove any scent that might reveal its presence to an enemy.

PEAT MOSS: an alternative to commercial cat litter for a cat's sanitary pan.

PEDIGREE: the record or official piece of paper that gives a cat's ancestral line.

PEDIGREED: a term for a cat that comes from at least three generations of pure *breeding*. When mated to another cat of the same *breed,* the results should be (but are not always) predictable.

PEKE-FACED PERSIAN: a red long-haired variety (first recognized in the United States) that is either a *Red Self* or a *Red Tabby*. The head should resemble the Pekingese dog; the nose should be short and depressed, the *muzzle* wrinkled.

PENCILINGS: the delicate face markings on *tabby* cats.

PERCHING INSTINCT: the instinct of a cat or kitten to climb and thus get away from any danger on the ground.

PERSIAN: The exact origin of the Persian cat is a bit murky. However, it is a fact that *long haired cats* have been known in Persia and Turkey for over three hundred years and it is speculated that the Crusaders brought them back from the Holy Wars. The most prevalent opinion is that the first long-haired cats came from Ankara, Turkey, and were called *Angoras*, and that the Persian cats from Persia, now Iran, came later. The original Angora had a narrower build, more slender head, longer nose and slightly shorter fur.

Today, due primarily to selective breeding, most long-haired cats are of the Persian type even though some of the blood is likely to be part Angora. (Some experts consider the words synonymous, though most separate the two. Many include both under the umbrella term "Long-haired Cat."

The ideal Persian type has a round, wide head, a very short nose, large round eyes contrasting to the coat color, and tufted ears. The legs should be sturdy, and shortish and the body *cobby*, that is, deep-chested, sturdy and somewhat squared. The tail should be short and fully furred.

A Persian in an attitude of curious expectancy.

"See how beautiful I am," this Silver Tabby Persian seems to be saying

The coat is of the utmost importance. It should be long, flowing and full. The fur should stand away from the body when brushed, forming a *frill,* or ruff, around the head

The Persian makes a beautiful majestic pet. In temperament some say it is placid; others that it is temperamental and nervous This undoubtedly depends on the strain and individual cat. It can be said, though, that these pampered looking creatures are a strong and sturdy breed. However, they must be combed religiously and daily for good looks and good health and some do resent handling (thing

Sapphire blue eyes in contrast to a champion Persian's pure-white coat.

Blue-Cream Persian with a wide, wide ruff.

The somewhat rare Sealpoint Persian. Same colors but completely different body type from the Siamese.

it is good to think about if one has small children).

There are numerous show varieties including the following: white with blue eyes (most of which are deaf), orange eyes or odd-colored eyes; black with orange or copper eyes; blue with orange or copper eyes; red with copper or deep orange eyes; cream with copper or orange eyes; chinchilla or silver with a brick red nose and green or blue-green eyes; smoke black, with a white undercoat and copper or orange eyes; blue smoke, similar to the above; *tortoiseshell*, with orange or copper eyes and a patched red, cream and black coat; *tortoiseshell and white*, or *calico*, similar to tortoiseshell but interspersed with white; shaded silver, with a delicate ticked coat and blue-green or green eyes; and the red, brown, blue and silver tabbies, with clear, distinct *tabby* facial and body markings and short, full ringed tails.

PERSPIRATION: moisture exuded from the pores. Cats perspire through their foot pads. A badly frightened cat leaves damp footprints behind.

Pure white Persian kittens on a rug that just might be their mother.

A mother cat knows how to get her kitten out of trouble, fast.

PET SHOPS: commercial shops where *pedigreed* and non-pedigreed cats and dogs, as well as other animals, are sold.

Investigate any pet shop before you buy. (Are the cages clean? How are the animals treated? What experiences have others had?) Try to get the owner to agree to let you take back the cat if it does not pass a veterinarian examination within several days.

For breeding purposes, the best stock is most likely to be acquired from a *breeder*. For pet purposes, it probably doesn't matter.

PICKING UP: Mother cats pick their kittens up by the *scruff* of the neck, but people shouldn't do so except in an emergency. (A cat of any age in a state of panic may have to be picked up that way.) The best way to pick up a cat is to slide one hand under the cat's body toward the front and support the hindquarters with the other hand. Lift and then tuck the cat parallel to your body. If you point

149

the head directly toward you the cat will instinctively claw to get a foothold. Cat's don't like to have their legs dangle.

PLAY: a necessary form of exercise and the main form for many housecats. Most cats are imaginative at improvising new games and all cats, particularly "only" cats, need regular play periods.

PLEASURE: Cats show pleasure by *purring, drooling, kneading* their paws, raising their hindquarters, rolling over, licking, "talking," leaping on laps, and showing they want to play with you.

PNEUMONIA: an acute and serious inflammation of the lung, which is likely to result in fever, breathing difficulties, and a cough. The cat may appear listless and not be hungry. Veterinary attention is likely to include *antibiotics*, and careful home *nursing* will be necessary. It is especially important to keep the convalescent cat warm and out of drafts.

POINTS: the darker coloring seen on the faces, paws, and tails of certain *breeds* such as *Siamese*.

A term also used for the marks given in shows for the various breeds. The number is always set at 100 for the ideal cat of any breed though the breakdown of points given for individual characteristics varies from breed to breed and from country to country.

POISONING: many household preparations are poisonous to cats. Among them are paints, many insect sprays, all coal tar products and some flea powders, turpentine, zinc ointment, and certain strong soaps, salves, and detergents.

Cats may also be accidently poisoned by chewing the leaves of plants that have been sprayed, catching mice and rats that have eaten poison, and by eating certain toxic plants such as laurel.

Prevention is better than any cure. Don't leave anything around in the house or garage that the cat might accidently get on its fur and then lick off or inhale, as when a room has been sprayed.

If you suspect poisoning (trembling, *vomiting,* and *fits* are symptoms) call the veterinarian right away.

POLYDACTYLISM: extra toes, a rather common hereditary characteristic.

POST-MORTEM EXAMINATION: an autopsy or after-death examination done to determine the cause of death. Through the examination of dead animals come advances in the treatment of other living cats and a greater knowledge about cat diseases.

POT BELLY: in kittens, a sign of *worms* or malnutrition; in grown cats, may be a sign of kidney trouble, a tumor, or a diseased uterus. See your veterinarian for a diagnosis.

PREGNANCY: The period of gestation, or pregnancy, in the cat (from copulation to birth) is normally around 65 days. There is likely to be no visible sign of pregnancy for the first four weeks. However, a trained person can tell whether the cat is pregnant between the third to the fifth week by gently feeling the abdominal wall for tell-tale lumps. By the sixth or seventh week, fullness in the sides is generally unmistakable.

A pregnant cat should be treated as normally as possible, not like a sick cat. She should be allowed a normal amount of exercise until she herself cuts down. Throughout most of the pregnancy she should be fed a normal well-balanced diet, plus the addition of non-fat milk or another calcium product. A *vitamin-mineral* supplement is also helpful. Toward the end of the pregnancy she should be fed smaller but more frequent meals.

During the last couple of weeks, especially if the cat seems to poke around the house, it may be wise to make a *kittening* box out of a cardboard grocery box. A suitable box or nest for kittening should have sides to keep the newborns from roaming, be sufficiently large, have shredded paper and toweling on the bottom, and be in a dark, quiet place, because the mother cat will prefer it and because light and confusion are not good for tiny kittens. In other words, you outfit the box and put it in a place the cat seems to prefer. Then you hope she will not decide your bed or stocking drawer is an even more suitable spot. It is likely her choice will be the final one. (See also *gestation, kittening*.)

PREGNANCY, FIRST SIGNS OF: a slight swelling of the nipples, which become a deeper pink. This should be noticeable three to four weeks after a successful mating.

PREGNANCY PROBLEMS: Following are two pregnancy problems: 1. Abortion: the premature expulsion of the unborn kittens from the mother cat's womb. It may be due to hormone imbalance, infection, a damaged placenta, or a hereditary inclination. 2. False Pregnancy: when the cat's nipples develop and there are other signs of pregnancy such as hunger and nest building but no forthcoming litter. The condition sometimes rèsults from the male's sterility or from the reabsorption of the embryos. Older cats are more subject to both conditions.

PREMIER: a show term for a *neutered pedigreed* cat the equal of a *champion entire* cat.

PROGNOSIS: a medical term for the prediction of the outcome of a disease or injury at the time of a diagnosis. Relevant factors are knowledge about the condition, veterinary experience, and other aspects about the cat such as age, temperament, and general health.

PROVERBS ABOUT CATS: There are many, including the English: "Curiosity killed the cat; satisfaction brought it back"; the Portuguese: "Wherever the mice laugh at the cat, there you will find a hole"; the French: "Whoever cares for cats well will marry as happily as he or she wishes"; and the universal: "When the cat is away, the mice will play."

PULSE: A normal cat's pulse beats between 100 and 130 times a minute. A fast pulse may accompany fever, *pneumonia, bleeding,* and *poisoning*, as well as *nervousness*. The pulse generally slows in old age.

PUMA: Also called Mountain Lion and Cougar, the Puma once ranged throughout most of North and South America; now it is most frequently found in the Canadian Rockies and the southwestern

The graceful, sure-footed Puma prefers a lofty perch.

United States. There are widely differing opinions about the Puma. Western ranchers have called it a cattle killer yet people have kept it successfully as a pet. Some say it is shy; others audacious. In appearance, the Puma looks a little like a small Lioness, its hindquarters are higher than its head and chest, while the body line is long and slender. Coat color is yellow-brown with lighter underparts.

Two things are certain about this intriguing animal: it is so powerfully built it can pull five times its own weight and it can leap up to 20 feet in one bound.

PUNISHMENT: Cats respond better to prevention than to punishment, and learn better by being rewarded rather than admonished. However, observation shows that mother cats chastise their kittens from time to time. (See also *training*.)

PUREBRED: a cat with the unadulterated blood of a particular breed. Even though matings of purebred cats are controlled, there is no reliable gauge as to whether the kittens will be exactly like the

Veteran cat actress (age: sixteen-plus and not telling) who appeared in the stock version of Bell, Book and Candle, *a part customarily played by a Siamese.*

parents in characteristics and temperament. Kittens have a way of being unpredictable.

PURRING: a low, continuous murmuring sound and a unique expression of felines to show contentment and joy, as well as occasionally pain. No one knows exactly how cats purr. The purrs of different cats vary in intensity and pitch.

PUSS: a colloquial name for the cat, which comes from the name of the cat-headed goddess of the ancient Egyptians called Pasht, who represented both good and evil.

PUSSY WILLOW AND CAT LEGEND: There is a legend that once many little kittens were thrown into a river to drown. The mother cat wept and was so distraught that the willows on the bank felt compassion and held out their branches to the struggling kittens. The little kittens clung to them and were saved. Ever since that time, each spring, the willow wears gray buds that feel as soft and silky as the coats of little kittens. Thus, the trees are called pussy willows.

PUTTING TO SLEEP: see *euthanasia*.

PYEWACKET: a name going back to medieval times. Used for the witch's *Siamese* cat in *Bell, Book and Candle*, it has been particularly popular ever since.

QUARANTINE: the isolation of animals, especially those coming from other countries or infested areas, to prevent the spread of disease.

Some countries require a guarantine, or isolation, period before a pet born elsewhere can live freely with its owners. Others may require certain shots or a health certificate. If moving or traveling abroad with a cat, check the quarantine regulations, which vary widely.

QUEEN: the term used for an unspayed female cat, especially one that has had or is about to have kittens.

QUICK: the top portion of a cat's claw, which is living tissue and contains blood vessels and nerves. This is the part that bleeds if you trim the *claws* too close. (In which case apply a mild *antiseptic* ointment, and then *bandage* the whole foot. If it doesn't heal, see your veterinarian.)

R

RABIES: a rare but always fatal disease, less common in the cat than in the dog. It does not exist in England because of a six-month quarantine on pets coming into the country.

If bitten by a vicious, highly excited cat, have it caught and tested. Otherwise your doctor may recommend a rather painful set of preventative shots for you.

There are several varieties of anti-rabies vaccination for cats, which many veterinarians recommend. Consult with him if your cat has been bitten by any animal suspected of having rabies. (Rats, skunks, squirrels, and bats occasionally carry the virus.)

RAGDOLL: a new variety of medium-sized, light colored cat with frost or seal *points*, a white stomach, blue eyes, and a tail carried like a plume. The significant thing about these cats is their disposition. Supposedly they can be picked up and handled even by strangers and will not fight or panic. It is said that they do not feel pain as other animals do. They are among the most affectionate, playful, and alert cats.

RAW MEAT, FEEDING: Raw meat is recommended by many experts as the best food because it is the cat's natural food in its natural condition. Others consider it good but not necessary. Horse meat, beef, lamb, and lamb kidney may all be served raw. Raw liver is fine but it sometimes has a laxative effect. Pork and fish should never be served raw, and all meat should be cooked if there is a question regarding its age or condition.

RECESSIVE: in *genetics*, the one of two possible traits that is usually masked; the opposite of dominant. (See also *dominant*.)

RED AMERICAN SHORT-HAIR: an all-red cat with a short, dense even coat of red (having no markings or shadings) and brilliant gold eyes. (See also *Domestic Short-Hair*).

RED-POINT: also called Red Colorpoint Short-Hair, the standard for the Red-Point is the same as for *Siamese*. The *points* should be all the same quality of color and all a deep, dark red; the body light. This is a relatively rare breed. (See also *Siamese*.)

RED SELF LONG-HAIR: unmarked (no white hairs or *tabby* stripes) full-coated *Persian* type cat with rich, deep red coat and deep copper eyes. It is rarely seen.

Red Tabby Long Hair

Siamese Red Point

Red Short Hair Domestic

RED TABBY: a typically Britis[h] type of _périgreed_ long or short haired cat. Red Tabbies should b[e] a real red in the background colo[r] with deeper red mahogany mark[-] ings. There should be no white i[n] the coat, and no marmalade color[-] ing.

When _purebred_ Red Tabbie[s] mate, kittens of both sexes wi[ll] likely be produced. When only on[e] parent is a Red Tabby, only th[e] male kittens are likely to be re[d.] Female kittens are likely to be _tor[-] toiseshells_. (See also _Mar[-] malade_.)

REFUSING FOOD: A cat ma[y] refuse food when it is feelin[g] finicky or has eaten elsewhere.

If you try several different kind[s] of food and the cat continues t[o] refuse to eat, especially if the ca[t] looks dull or unwell, or if the ca[t] keeps sniffing eagerly but doesn['t] eat, consult with a veterinarian[.] The cat may be ill or may hav[e] an obstruction.

REGISTRATION OF BREEDS[:] the filling out of a form by a register[-] ing cat association (upon receip[t] of a fee) which gives the projecte[d] name and complete geneologica[l] history of a _pedigreed_ cat or kitten[.] Once registered, a record is kep[t] and the cat's name and numbe[r] cannot be changed even if it is sol[d] to a new owner. In England, ther[e] is one registering group. There ar[e] a number in the States. The sam[e] name cannot be used for 20 years[.]

RELIGION AND CATS: The ca[t] was worshipped as a god i[n] ancient Egypt and later venerate[d] by the Romans and Orientals. Ca[t] worship was so prevalent i[n] Europe that Pope Innocent VIII, a[t]

the end of the 15th century, ordered the Inquisition to search out and burn cat worshippers as witches.

Happily the cat survived, though now it is considered more a beloved pet and symbol of liberty than a god.

REPELLANTS: special commercial cat preparations to keep cats off furniture and so forth. Their effectiveness is debatable.

REX: a sport, or *mutation*, of the domestic cat, the Rex has a soft and silky curly coat rather than a straight one; therefore it is sometimes called the "poodle" cat.

The first Rex was born in Cornwall, England, and was mated back to his mother, which established the strain which then became a *breed*. The descendants are called Cornish Rex.

A second cat with a curly coat but from entirely different ancestors appeared in Devon, in 1960, and eventually established the strain known as Devon Rex.

Both types have only one thick top coat, with no undercoat or guard hairs. The Devon Rex has a slightly thinner coat and a more slender body. The Cornish Rex is built along squarer, cobbier lines. Rex cats may be of any color.

As a pet, the Rex is intelligent, affectionate, and outgoing. Because it has a quiet voice and loving temperament and doesn't shed, this rather rare breed makes an ideal house cat.

Rex

157

RHEUMATISM: joint diseases including *arthritis*, occurring mainly in older cats. Lameness and stiffness are symptoms. See your veterinarian.

RICKETS: a debilitating disease caused by the lack of sufficient absorption of calcium and phosphorus, which inhibits normal bone growth.

Stray kittens often have rickets —short bowed legs, lumps along the ribs, and dull, drab coats.

Care and *vitamin* therapy usually helps. A veterinarian can advise.

RIGHTING: what a cat does when it falls. Instinctively it turns so that it lands on its feet.

RINGWORM: Ringworm is caused by a fungus not a *worm* and affects man and cat alike. Either can give it to the other.

Symptoms in the cat are bald spots; symptoms in humans are itchiness and blotchiness. While ringworm tends to spread and is highly contagious, it is relatively easy to cure. If you and the cat have similar symptoms, see both a doctor and a veterinarian. Treatment inculdes the use of fungicides and sometimes of ultraviolet light.

ROAMING: Cats are natural hunters and most cats allowed outdoors will stray to other yards in search of prey. Some, especially *tomcats*, are prone to wander away for days.

Although the cat is a nervous animal, it is not prone to dizziness. When turned over and dropped, it rights itself instinctively with agility and precision.

Neutering the cat at an early age usually cuts down on roaming, and collaring helps to ensure the return of a pet.

Cats that roam excessively generally have shorter lives. (See also *cats and the law*.)

RODENTS AS CAT FOOD: No cat should live only on the rodents it catches. Moreover, many rats are diseased and can kill a cat or make it very sick. (See also *mousers*.)

RODENT ULCERS: lesions supposedly caused by rat bites, first appearing on the lip and sometimes spreading to other parts of the body. Rodent ulcers sometimes respond slowly to treatment. See your veterinarian, who will recommend the proper ointments and drugs.

R.S.P.C.A.: initials standing for the Royal Society for the Prevention of Cruelty to Animals, which is responsible for animal welfare throughout the United Kingdom.

RUFF: see *frill*.

RUNT: The runt of the litter is noticeably the smallest one. It also may be the most active. The energetic runt that pushes its way to the milk supply will likely make an unusually intelligent, delightful, and healthy adult cat. The opposite is true if the cat is smallest because of disease or a congenital difficulty.

RUSSIAN BLUE: also called Foreign Blue, American Blue, *Maltese*, or just Blue, these are fine-boned, long-bodied, exceptionally graceful cats with wedge-shaped faces, rather flat skulls, large, pointed, almost transparent ears, dainty oval feet and prominent whiskers. They have double coats

Russian Blue

with a silvery, sealskin texture. The fur should be thick and close and the same clear blue shade all over. White hairs and *tabby* markings are faults. The eyes should be a vivid green; the tail long and tapering.

There are numerous stories and legends about their origin including one that alleges that they once were the palace cats of the Tzars. Actually, it is more likely that they are a sport rather than of actual Russian background.

The Russian Blue is an unusually agile and fearless cat. On the other hand, it is gentle and quiet, takes to leads relatively easily, and makes a loyal, lovable pet.

RUSTY-SPOTTED CAT: a small, elegant cat weighing about three pounds that resembles the *Leopard Cat* and lives in India and Ceylon. It is rust to tawny in color, with white underparts, and is said to be easily tamed when taken young.

Rusty-spotted Cat

S

SAFETY PRECAUTIONS: Use screens on high windows. Use only stretch *collars* around the cat's neck. Carefully read labels of rodent and insect *poisons* before using; many are highly toxic. Keep household cleaning equipment out of the cat's reach as some are poisonous. Keep the sewing box closed, needles and pins picked up. Watch out for broken glass and also for open drawers, trunks, dryers, and closets the cat might accidently get shut up in.

SALIVATING: see *drooling*.

SAND CAT: a North African yellow to gray brown cat with wide apart ears, thickly-furred paws, and large, expressive eyes. There is little known about the Sand Cat except that it hides and bears its young in sand burrows.

SCANDANAVIA, CATS IN: Cats have always played a large part in Scandanavian legend and folk lore, though interest in breeding and shows has been belated, owing in part to the extremely cold winters, which necessitate keeping *stud* cats indoors.

SCOTTISH FOLD: a mutated variety of short-coated, any-colored cat with downward folding ears, now seen in several countries.

SCRATCHING POST: All cats need to scratch their *claws* along sharp surfaces to sharpen them. This is cat nature as the claws are a prime form of protection. Also, the scratching is an important form of exercise.

Whatever kind of scratching post is used—plain rough bark or a *catnip*-scented, carpeted post—it should be introduced while the cat is a tiny kitten. It should be close to where the cat sleeps and the cat should be encouraged to use it by having its paws put on the post whenever it tries to scratch elsewhere. A spring toy attached to the top will make it more attractive. The main thing is that the kitten must be constantly and consistently shown the purpose of the post in the very first months of its life. (See also *declawing*.)

SCRUFF: the loose skin at the back of the neck by which the mother cat picks up one of her kittens.

SEEING: see *eyesight*.

SELF-COLORED: a cat with the same color all over without any markings.

SERVAL: a brownish cat with black spots from the African bush

A catnip mouse will more likely make the cat want to use its scratching post.

country. The Serval is about three and a half feet long and makes an affectionate pet if taken as a kitten.

Serval

SEXING: To tell the sex of a kitten, hold the kitten in the palm of your one hand and lift the tail with the other. The openings are farther apart in the male than in the female; a half inch apart in newborn male kittens, a quarter inch apart in female kittens. The effect is one of two separated dots (a colon) in the male; a line and a dot (an exclamation point) in the female. At about eight weeks the male organs appear as a soft bunch between the two openings while the female remains flat. In adult altered cats, the male has a tiny round opening for the penis, one to one-and-a-half inches below the anus, while the female has a vertical slit about a half inch below the anus.

SHADED SILVER: a long-haired *Persian* type cat with a pure, unmarked, but heavily *ticked* coat, giving the effect of a mantle shad-

Shaded Silver

ing down the face, sides, legs, and tail. The rims of the eyes should be outlined in black; the nose should be a brick-red. Any brown tinge or tracing of bars is considered a fault although kittens often have *tabby* stripes which fade as they grow older.

SHEDDING: the dropping of a cat's hair, more profuse in spring and summer. Excessive shedding may be a sign of *nervousness*, impending illness, or a tempera-

ture change. In general, the more a cat sheds, the more *brushing* it needs.

SHOCK: a serious state usually following an accident or severe *bleeding*. The animal's circulatory responses are lowered, the limbs collapse, the lips become pale and the body may feel cold. All a layman should do is cover the cat with a blanket and call a veterinarian right away.

SHOWING A CAT: every association has its own particular forms and procedures. However, some things might be mentioned if you intend to show your cat. It should learn to be accustomed to a pen long before the show. It should be in perfect coat. It should not be fed within several hours of taking it to the show. Afterwards, it should be taken home as quickly as possible and kept away from other cats for at least a week, on the off chance that it might have picked up a germ. Some experts recommend giving it a mild *antiseptic* mouth rinse; others a mild milk and brandy.

SHOWS: where cats are judged according to set standards which vary from country to country and sometimes from association to association. The most important season is usually from September to February for several reasons: *long-haired cats* are not in full coat in spring and summer, unaltered females are likely to be having kittens in the spring and summer and consequently unaltered male cats will be harder to handle if the females are in season.

SIAMESE: Siamese are among the most exotic and interesting of

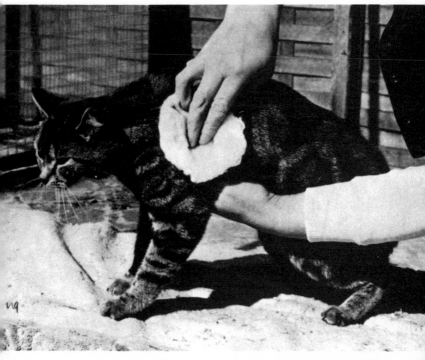

A show cat may be wiped with a chamois cloth to give its coat an even more perfect sheen.

all cats. Most but not all authorities agree that they originated in Siam, where, according to one story, they were bred and the type fixed by the father of a Siamese king. (At one time the penalty for a commoner stealing one of the royal cats was death.) When first imported, as early as 1870, in England, they were rather delicate. Now they are among the most sturdy of cats and are the most popular short-haired breed.

A good Siamese cat is lithe and elegant, clever and loyal. It has a

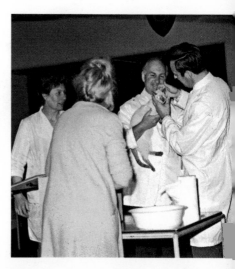

A contender being checked by a veterinarian before being judged.

Sealpoint Siamese kittens: brother and sister.

Sealpoint Siamese in a typical attitude of alert responsiveness.

Lilac Point Siamese in repose.

Lilac Point Siamese, mother and kittens.

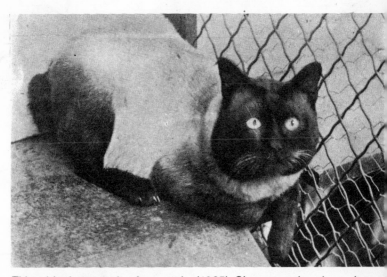

This old photograph of an early (1905) Siamese prizewinner has a cobby, squarish build, looking little like today's sleek Siamese and proving that breeds do change.

lean body, alert ears topping a wedge-shaped face, and almond-shaped, sapphire blue eyes. The coat should be short, fine, and glossy; the body color uniform and contrasting with the darker color of the points: the face mask, ears, feet, legs and tail. The varieties of Siamese are seal-point: brown on a light cream body; chocolate-point: milk chocolate contrasting with an ivory body; lilac-point: pink gray on an off-white body; blue or frost point: gray-blue on a pure white body; red point: red gold on a whitish body; and *tabby*-point: a pale, unmarked body with silver and black tabby markings on the face, legs and tail. (The latter is relatively rare and is not recognized everywhere.)

When Siamese kittens of any variety are born, they are almost

Chocolate Point Siamese

The Silver Tabby has very distinct markings of black on pale silver.

pure ivory in color. The points deepen as the cat grows older. Female Siamese kittens tend to mature sexually earlier than other cats and Siamese *queens* often like their owners around during *kittening*.

Other Siamese traits are an unusually expressive vocabulary, a heightened dependence on humans, adaptability to a collar and leash, dislike of medicine, quick wits, stubbornness, loyalty to their humans, and a jealous, clever, sensitive, affectionate nature. Because they are so intelligent and amusing and people loving, Siamese cats make excellent pets. (See also *American standards*.)

SILVER TABBY: a coloring found in both long- and short-haired cats. The background color should be a pure, pale silver with no tinge of brown; the *tabby* markings a jet-black and predominant as possible. Eyes should be hazel or green. The body type should, for show purposes, conform to the length of hair, a requirement which doesn't matter a whit for a pet or artistic purposes as a Silver Tabby of any type is one of the most beautiful cats. Moreover, it has an innately healthy body and an unusually

lively, alert, affectionate disposition.

SIX SENSE: second sight and a way of knowing beyond the usual five senses. The sixth sense includes homing ability and the ability to forecast and predict events. Cats definitely have the former and occasionally seem to have the latter. In such instances, as when a cat reacted to a murder ahead of time, there is no telling whether it was a matter of sixth sense or an unusual heightening of one of the ordinary senses. There is also an unproven belief that cats have a sixth sense about when they are going to die.

Silver Tabby

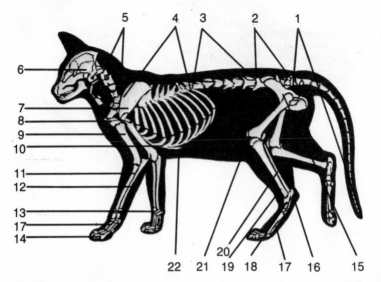

Skeleton **1.** *Caudal or Tail Bones* **2.** *Siacra Bones* **3.** *Lumbar Bones* **4.** *Dorsal or Thoracic Bones* **5.** *Cervical or Neck Bones* **6.** *Cranium* **7.** *Scapula or Shoulder Blade* **8.** *Clavicle or Collar Bone* **9.** *Humerus* **10.** *Sternum* **11.** *Radius* **12.** *Ulna* **13.** *Carpal or Wrist Bone* **14.** *Phalanges or Toes* **15.** *Pelvis or Hip Bone* **16.** *Calcis or Heel Bone* **17.** *Metatarsa. (Rear) Metacarpal (Front Bones)* **18.** *Tarsal Bone* **19.** *Tibia* **20.** *Fibula* **21.** *Patella or Knee Cap* **22.** *Costal Cartilages*

Cheetah Skull

Leopard Skull

SKELETON: the bony structure that forms the framework of the body. The bones both support and protect. The bones of the limbs and spinal column act as levers upon which the muscles pull, thus facilitating movement. (See also *anatomy*.)

SKIN: A cat has an extremely flexible, mobile skin, which enables it to easily slip away from an enemy.

SKULL: The bony frame around the head which supports the face and within which the brain is enclosed and protected.

SMELL: The sense of smell is highly refined in the cat, who uses its nose to sniff out a mouse hole, find a mate, and simply to enjoy the subtle odors of *catnip, flowers,* and certain perfumes. A cat always sniffs its food as part of its pleasure in it. A cat with a respiratory problem may temporarily lose its appetite. A cat may refuse to eat if its dish has been cleaned in a smelly disinfectant or it may snub a person whose odor it doesn't like.

SMOKE: a variety of long-haired *Persian* type cat that is extremely handsome and is called "a cat of contrasts" due to its unusual black

Smoke

fur with a white undercoat, black face mask, silver tufted ears, and expressive round copper or orange eyes. The kittens are born black, the white in the coat showing later. There is also a blue variety of Smoke.

SNOW LEOPARD: also called Ounce, there is some debate as to whether the Snow Leopard is one of the roaring cats and as to what family it belongs. (The other roaring cats are *Lion, Tiger, Leopard,* and *Jaguar*.) There is no debate, however, that it is an exceedingly beautiful and increasingly rare pale gray to yellow, rather long-haired Wild Cat with a white belly and bushy rosette-marked tail. It ranges from Russia to Tibet and from the Himalayas to the Atlas Mountains into China, preferring the land between the tree line and the permanent snow line.

SNUB: a term for the short, flat noses seen in some *long-haired* varieties.

SOUTH AFRICA, CATS IN: There are a number of *cat clubs* in South Africa grouped together under one governing council. There is an extremely interested *cat fancy*, and shows are held in different

Snow Leopard

parts of the country. While the Siamese is most popular, there is an increased interest in some of the more unusual *breeds*.

SPAYING: the surgical removal of the uterus and ovaries of the female cat. It is generally done when the cat is between four and five months old because the cat owner does not want the responsibility of kittens or the social problems associated with heat and the loud calling of the female.

The operation is relatively serious (more so as the cat ages) and relatively expensive, but is almost always successful, even when the female cat is older and has already had kittens. In the latter case, spaying should be done after the milk has dried up.

It is sometimes possible to spay a pregnant cat. Consult with your veterinarian.

SPECIES: There are 51 species of "Felis," the generic term for cats.

SPOTTED CATS: known also as *Leopard Cats* and Spotted Tabbies, they are relatively rare today. The more spots and the more distinct the better. Background colors are brown, red, yellow, and blue; eye color should conform. Tabby pencil markings are faults.

SPRAYING: what an unaltered *tomcat* does to define its territory and attract a female. The spraying may be disastrously accurate and the odor is unfortunately strong and sickening to humans, which is one reason why all but *stud* male cats are normally *altered*. (Only occasionally due to overstimulation or emotional disturbance does an altered male spray.)

SQUINT: an inclination to crossed eyes, a hereditary characteristic in some *Siamese* cats. The eyeballs do not move in a coordinated way though this does not seem to affect the visual power of the cat.

STIFLE: the hind leg joint, corresponding to the human knee.

STOMACH: After a cat has eaten its stomach is roughly the size of a closed fist. The membranes are resiliant, though domestic cats have a tendency to stomach disorders. The stomach is also the most sensitive area of a cat and a wild cat instinctively protects it. If a cat rolls over displaying its stomach you can be sure it trusts you.

STOP: a slight depression between the forehead and nose of some long-haired *Persian*-type cats.

STRAY: a cat without a home. It may have left home on its own, been abandoned, or gotten lost while hunting or being chased. (Some cats seem to have something in their temperament that makes them want to wander.) If a stray cat comes up to you, it is evidence that it has once had a home. Genuine strays are tough and aloof and will not approach people. Take the stray to the nearest animal shelter, post notices, and try to find its rightful owner. If you become its next owner, take it to a veterinarian for a checkup.

STUD: a male cat used for *breeding* purposes.

SUNSHINE: Cats love sunshine and it is an excellent source of Vitamin D, which helps kill germs and prevent skin infections.

SUPERSTITIONS ABOUT CATS:
Most anti-cat superstitions originated around the time of the Inquisition. Some of these false sayings were that a cat has nine lives, sucks a baby's breath, and that a black cat brings bad luck if it crosses in front of you because it is a witch's cat.

Conversely white, *calico*, and *tortoiseshell* cats are supposed to bring good luck, as are black cats according to legend in some areas.

According to one American hill-country superstition, a cat can decide whether or not a girl should get married. The debating bride-to-be takes three hairs from the cat's tail and wraps them in a paper, which she then puts under her doorstep. If the cat hairs are arranged in a Y pattern the next morning, her answer is "yes"; if an N pattern, it is "no."

SWIM, ABILITY TO: All cats can swim in dog-paddle fashion, but few domestic varieties, except for the Turkish cat, act as if they enjoy it. A number of wild varieties, including *Lions* and *Tigers* play in water and chase their prey in it.

SWITZERLAND, CATS IN: There are comparatively few *pedigreed* Swiss cats. But the ones that exist have won numerous prizes, especially in the *long-haired* field.

A Turkish cat swimming for the pure pleasure of it.

T

TABBY: The word "tabby" comes from the Arabian "attabi," which was a kind of wavy-lined silk produced in Old Baghdad. The tabby pattern of stripes and bars is found on both common and *purebred* cats and is said to be the original coat pattern of cats. In addition, it is said that if all the cats in the world intermated, their offspring would all be tabbies, as the pattern is dominant over all others.

In the classic tabby pattern, the markings are dense and clearly defined and somewhat broad, with swirls on the cheeks and sides.

In the mackerel tabby pattern, the markings are narrower and run

A tiger-striped tabby with a pillow much like himself. Tabbies are alert, affectionate and always amusing.

around the body in stripes. This is the pattern sometimes called "Tiger."

There are varied colors of both long- and short-haired tabby cats. The silver tabby has black markings on a clear pale or silver background. The markings of the brown tabby are also black but the back-

Macheral Tabby

ground color is a rich tawny brown. In the blue tabby, the background color is a pale bluish ivory, and the markings are a dense dark blue, while the cream tabby has a pale cream background color, with deeper markings of the same color. Finally, the red tabby has a background color of clear red, and dense, deeper red markings.

TAIL: The cat's tail is actually an extension of its spinal column. It uses its tail for balance and as a means of expression to "talk" and to signal other cats and humans. The different breeds have different desired tail shapes.

TALKING: see *language*.

TAPEWORMS: see *worms*.

TARTAR: the brownish-yellow deposit that forms on a cat's teeth, which may be soft or hard, and under which decay starts. Tartar is always a sign of trouble.

TEATS: the nipples projecting from the breast that enable kittens to suck and get milk from their mother. Each teat normally has a number of openings through which the milk flows. Occasionally a condition called "blind teats" occurs in which there are no openings. The milk builds up and then the mammary gland dries up and a *foster mother* must be found.

TEETH: Every normal cat has two sets of teeth. The first are called milk teeth and are shed between four and seven months (six is average). Teething occasionally causes *fits*, in which case put the kitten in a basket in a darkened room and call the veterinarian.

The adult teeth number 30: 12 sharp front incisors for shearing, 4 canines for spearing and 14 molars and premolars in the back.

The cat uses its teeth to fight, bite and kill prey, and to tear and

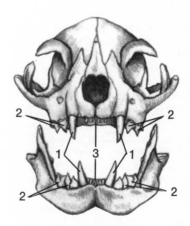

1. *Canines* **2.** *Incisors* **3.** *Premolars and Molars*

173

cut food although a cat does not chew as we do.

Tooth troubles generally occur as a cat gets older. Tartar deposits, foul breath, and pawing at the mouth are symptoms of trouble. Too much mushy food isn't good. Give a cat some hard, crunchy food to help scrape off the tartar. An older cat should have its teeth examined regularly at home or professionally.

TELEGONY: the supposed influence of a previous *stud* on a mother cat's next litter. In other words, the belief that if a *pedigreed* cat mates with a common cat, this will somehow spoil the purity of future litters. It is a totally mistaken belief.

TEMPERATURE: The normal temperature of the cat is 101.5 degrees. Factors other than illness may affect it—age, sex, outside temperature, amount of exercise. A degree one way or the other is no cause for alarm in an otherwise normal cat.

It is important to know how to take a cat's temperature when the veterinarian asks and when there are symptoms such as severe *vomiting* or *diarrhea*. Use a rectal thermometer well lubricated with white petroleum jelly or mineral oil. Preferably have a helper to hold the cat. The cat may be in a upright or reclining position. Lift the tail and insert with a rotary movement. Firm pressure may have to be applied to get the thermometer in the needed one to one and a half inches. The cat may cry out, but don't be unnerved. It is more likely due to lost dignity than pain. Take out after one to three minutes. If the temperature is above 103, call the veterinarian.

THIRD EYELID OR HAW: the *nictitating membrane* at the inner corner of a cat's eye. Normally it is hidden by the lower eyelid, but it can be drawn across the eye at will to protect it from dust and grit. A membrane that suddenly protrudes and stays that way can be a symptom of illness, *worms, anemia*, or a general run-down condition. See your veterinarian.

THROWBACK: a cat that reverts back to characteristics found in long-gone ancestors but not in recent generations, due to a recombining of the genes.

TICKING: In referring to a cat's fur, ticking is a touch or tip of one color on the end of a hair of another color, as a brown hair with a black tip. "No ticking" as a standard means that each hair should be completely of one color.

TICKS: blood sucking *parasites* that attach themselves to furry animals. Cats that walk in the woods should be examined regularly for ticks. Ticks burrow into the flesh. If you find one, don't try to pull it with your bare hands. Swab it first with alcohol or chloroform to loosen its grip; then lift it away intact with tweezers. Afterwards make sure you destroy it by burning or dropping into the alcohol bottle.

TIGER: a large and beautiful member of the cat family who lives primarily in Asia. Tiger numbers are diminishing due to man's destruction of its habitat. The Tiger can adapt equally to cold and hot climates and is thought to have originated in Siberia. The biggest

A tiger in a contemplative mood, one of the most majestic of all animals.

Tigers still are found there and may be over 12 feet long and weigh over 600 pounds. The background color of the Tiger varies from red-orange to white but is always marked with distinctive black stripes. Tigers are good swimmers and excellent hunters. Most experts believe their reputation as man killers is exaggerated and that they will not attack humans unless provoked, ill, or protecting young.

TIGER CAT: a small South and Central American Wild Cat also called the Little Spotted Cat, similar to the *Margay* and the *Ocelot*. The main difference is that the stripes on its forehead and the spots on the rest of its body are less distinct. The Tiger Cat has white lines around the eyes, a dark ringed tail, and a yellowish basic coat color. Tiger Cats do not make reliable pets.

TIGLON: the name for an animal whose father is a *Lion* and mother is a *Tiger*. Tiglons cannot reproduce themselves. (See also *Liger*.)

TIME SENSE: Cats often seem to have an acute sense of time, knowing when their owners are coming home and when the stores where they work close. Cats rarely get locked out, but no one knows just how their inner "clocks" work.

TOMCAT: a common name for an unaltered male cat.

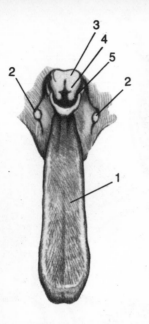

grooming, stimulating newborn kittens, and grasping food.

TONKANESE: a short-haired medium-sized cat being developed in England, which is the result of a mating of a *Siamese* with a *Burmese*.

TORTOISESHELL: an unusually attractive cat that is patched in distinct areas of red, black, and cream, generally the accidental result of mating self-colored cats. Tortoiseshell cats are almost invariably female and the occasional male is sterile. The patchings should be precise, defined and balanced, particularly on the face; the colors should be bright and clear. White hairs in the patches and solid-colored legs are faults. The eyes should be deep

TONGUE: The cat's tongue is vital for both eating and cleaning. The underside is smooth but the upper part is covered by tiny microsopic claw-shaped hooks useful for

Tortoiseshell.

176

copper or orange. A red mark called a blaze that runs from the forehead to the nose is an added asset. Tortoiseshell cats may be of the long-haired or short-haired type. Moreover there is a Blue Tortoiseshell variety in which the blue replaces the black. Probably because of so much cross-breeding, Tortoiseshell cats are known for their intelligence, good health, and playful ways. They are also supposed to be lucky.

TORTOISESHELL AND WHITE: long or short-haired cat similar to the tortoiseshell, with the addition of white. They are commonly called *Calico* cats. They are female and supposed to be lucky. The markings should be well-balanced and an excess of white is a fault. Both long and short haired varieties should conform to body type.

TOUCH: Many experts think that the cat has the most delicate sense of touch in the animal kingdom through its finely tuned whiskers and eyebrows and its probing paws. Cats tentatively touch strange objects, knead the laps of people they love, and touch *whiskers* with each other in meeting.

TOYS: Cats are imaginative in their play. They toy with a ribbon as if it were a snake, a paper wad as if it were a mouse, and an empty carton as if it were a tree house to attack and explore. Pet shops carry many suitable cat toys, often

A Siamese kitten playing catch.

177

A ball of yarn is a playmate you can really unwind with.

filled with *catnip*. In general cats love climbing, swinging, and spring toys, anything that moves or can be explored. A cat should not play with any toy with sharp edges or tiny swallowable parts, short strings, rubber bands, or anything connected with sewing (as cats have an unfortunate affinity for needles).

TRAINING: If you want to have a well-trained cat, the essential things are to start when the cat is a tiny kitten (cats born and reared in homes are more trainable than those reared in *catteries*), reward the cat for desired behavior (even if accidental), rather than punish it for wrong doing, and be consistent in words and approach. A cat

should never be shouted at, struck, or have its nose put in a mess.

Training periods should be brief and before the cat's dinner. Keep showing the cat where it should go and what it should do. Use a firm but friendly tone. Actually most cats train themselves to use the litter box and to recognize their names; the problems lie in training the cat to stay away from forbidden places and to use a scratching post. Beyond these basics, the *breeds* vary in their ability to be trained to a leash and to heel (which almost no *Persians* can). Individuals vary too, even in the same litter.

Keep in mind that some problems can be avoided by shutting doors, buying cut *flowers* the cat doesn't behead in its enthusiasm, and using *mothballs* and special *repellents*. Finally, if you have to quickly deter your cat or a visiting cat from the roast or uncaged canary, a loud handclap or glass of water tossed at the offender will probably do the trick. (See also *tricks* and *scratching post*.)

TRAVEL WITH A CAT: Cats vary in their ability to travel. Some love it, some are philosophical about it, other despise it. Try to accustom a cat to short jaunts before setting out on a long trip. Several hints: A large-enough enclosed, well-ventilated carrier or basket is a must (preferably closed with a padlock as cats are masters at undoing latches); most trains insist on them and a cat loose in a car is dangerous. The cat should not be fed for at least 12 hours before the trip. It should have access to water along the way. Bedding in the basket and a toy will make the trip more bearable. Talking to it helps sooth an anxious cat.

A recommended motion sickness remedy should be given to cats that get carsick (also spread papers about). Give the cat half a tablet about half an hour before setting out and more later if needed. Tranquilizers recommended by a veterinarian should be given really nervous cats. For airplane and ship travel, check with the particular line. Some allow a specified number of small pets in the cabin on a first-call, first served basis. Since all cats suffer some stress in moving, the best idea

might be to leave the pet at home with a caring and careful neighbor.

TREATS AND TIDBITS: Whether a snippet of cheese, a grape, a few flakes of cereal, or a commercial product, any extraordinary food the cat loves should be given only occasionally and in small amounts. Treats can be used on special occasions and as rewards for learning tricks.

TRICKS: amusing antics to please people, which most cats think are below their dignity. Some cats learn tricks more easily than others; sometimes from other cats. Nothing will force a reluctant cat to learn a trick. A cat will learn what or when it wants to. Brief training

Sitting up is a a nice trick and this American Short-Hair can do it.

periods, rewards, warm praise, and a consistent approach are most likely to succeed.

One trick on your part is to praise and reward the cat for what it does naturally, such as rolling over if that is what you want it to do on command. If you want a cat to learn to "shake," hold its paw, say "shake," and reward it with a tidbit. Go through the same routine in sessions lasting a few minutes. Every day, increase the time between the shake and the tidbit. Hopefully the cat will eventually raise its paw at the command alone. The same principle applies to teaching the cat to retrieve, jump on your shoulder, clap paws, jump through a hoop, or anything else. (See also *training*.)

TUFTS: the hairs growing from the ears or between the toes of a cat.

TURKISH CAT: a charming new variety of *long-haired cats*, also called Van cats as they are from that part of Turkey. Similar to the original *Angora* type, Turkish cats

Turkish Cat

have wedged-shaped heads, well-furred ears, and exceptionally thick, long coats, which they partly lose in the summer. The color is white with auburn markings on the faces and ears and auburn rings on the tails. The eyes are a distinctive light amber with pinkish rims. Turkish cats are unusual in that they appear to swim for the pure pleasure of it.

TYPE: a word used in *cat fancy* to denote a particular kind of body such as *Persian, British, American,* or *Foreign*.

V

VACCINATION: an inoculation with a vaccine to protect an animal from disease. Two of the dread cat diseases, *feline distemper* and *pneumonia*, can usually be warded off by vaccination by a veterinarian. Vaccination for feline distemper is particularly important and should be given when a kitten is six and ten weeks old. Booster shots are needed afterwards. Check with your veterinarian.

VACUUM CLEANER: The use of a vacuum cleaner's soft brush attachment is an odd but easy way to remove loose cat hairs. Many cats love being vacuumed.

VAGINA: the passage leading to the cervix in the female cat. Infection in the area is indicated by futile attemps to urinate and by licking. Veterinary treatment includes *antibiotics* and is usually successful.

VAN CAT: See *Turkish Cat*.

VEGETABLES: While cats are natural meat eaters, a pot of grass to nibble on or a daily spoonful or two of cooked vegetables (excluding potatoes) are good for adult cats and help regulate digestion and prevent *hairballs*.

Next to its owner, the veterinarian is a cat's best friend.

VETERINARIAN: a man or woman professionally trained in the medical and surgical treatment of animals, especially domestic animals. Choose a veterinarian of good reputation, one you trust, one that likes cats and handles them well, and ideally, one that is close by. (You should also ask if he or she makes house calls and has

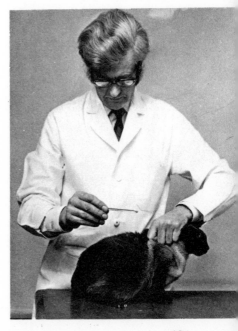

181

24-hour emergency service.) When explaining your cat's symptoms, be as detailed and explicit as possible. Then follow your veterinarian's instructions to the letter, no matter how time-consuming or inconvenient.

VIBRASSE: the stiff *whiskers* growing out of a cat's *muzzle*. These are sensory organs with finely tuned roots, which set off vibratory stimulations and send messages to the cat's brain, enabling even a blindfolded cat to put its feet firmly on a table though only its whiskers have touched the edges.

VICIOUSNESS: usually a result of cruelty, occasionally of heredity or overspoiling.

VIRUS: minute micro-organisms which live in cells and often cause diseases such as *feline distemper*.

VITAMINS AND MINERALS: any of a group of organic substances needed for good health and normal metabolism. The essential supplements for kittens are calcium, phosphorous, and Vitamin D. Adult cats need Vitamin A for good night vision, B for growth, as well as D and E, and certain minerals such as iron and iodine. Adult cats may be given special pet products or one-a-day human vitamins. Bonemeal is a fine supplementary source of calcium, especially needed for pregnant and nursing cats. *Yeast* is high in B vitamins and most cats like it.

VOMITING: regurgitation is common and happens for a variety of reasons: *worms,* a *hairball,* an obstruction, a tumor, *poisoning, constipation,* illness, overfeeding, over-excitement, or eating food that is too cold or too hot. In general, vomiting long after a meal is a more serious sign than vomiting immediately afterwards. A cat's stomach tends to reject anything that is indigestible. Examine the vomit to get an idea of what is wrong. Do you see matted hair, worms, a foreign object? Does the cat also act sick and feverish? In the latter case, call the veterinarian right away. Otherwise, give the cat a mild recommended motion sickness or stomach settling tablet or a teaspoon of milk of magnesia. Don't give it food or water for 24 hours. If it continues to vomit or refuses to eat, call the veterinarian.

W

WATER: Clean fresh water is essential to all cats. Change it at least once a day.

WEANING: accustoming a kitten to food other than its mother's milk: to supplementary milk (cow's milk made double strength by the addition of evaporated milk or powdered milk), or a special pet preparation, and/or solid food (baby food or finely cut up bits of raw or cooked meat).

The weaning process should be gradual and should begin when the kittens are three or four weeks old. They should be encouraged to lap milk and should be offered small portions of solid food. When they are five or six weeks old, at least two of their meals should be meat. At this age many kittens only suckle at night. By six to eight weeks, the kittens should be completely independent of the mother cat as a source of food, having five or six meals a day, alternately milk and meat based. (See also *feeding, kitten*.)

WEDGE: the characteristic head shape of *Siamese* and *Foreign* or *Oriental* varieties.

WEIGHT: On the average, a female adult cat should weigh between six and ten pounds, a

All cats must have daily fresh water.

male between eight to fifteen pounds. Some fat cats weigh up to 35 pounds. (See also *obesity*.)

WHIP: a long, slender tapering tail.

WHISKERS: A cat's whiskers, called *vibrassae*, are an important part of its sensory apparatus. They are delicate organs that enable even a blind cat to judge distances and surfaces. A cat tries the size of a hole by its whiskers; if they bend back, the cat won't go in. Never cut a cat's whiskers.

183

WHITE CATS, PUREBRED:
There are several varieties of long and short haired white cats. All are relatively rare and difficult to breed true and all are supposed to bring their owners good fortune. The coat should be pure white with no black hairs; the eyes sapphire blue, orange, or copper. It should be remembered that a large number of blue-eyed cats are born deaf. (Although they are not of show quality, white cats with green eyes make equally lovely and loveable pets.)

There are three recognized varieties of *long-haired* white or *Persian* cats: those with orange eyes, those with blue eyes (they are less likely to be deaf if born with a few black hairs) and those with odd eyes, a hereditary characteristic considered lucky.

Purebred short-haired white cats come in both *Foreign* slim-bodied types and *cobby,* British types. In both, the fur should be short and glossy and should lie close to the body. Finally, an *albino Siamese* cat has recently been bred, with typical Siamese characteristics but not with pink eyes.

WHITE TIGER: an *albino* strain of *Tiger* found in India.

WILL OF PET OWNER: A thoughtful pet owner might outline in his or her will what should be done with the cat in case of the owner's death. The person to care for the cat should be named and funds provided if possible.

WITCHCRAFT AND CATS: Cats have sometimes been associated with black magic and the devil. The Christian Church was anti-cat because so many pagan religions had worshipped the cat. In Europe, during the fourteenth and fifteenth centuries cats were denigrated, said to be sorcerers' pets and participants in Black Sabbaths. While in the witches' "Bible," formulas were given using cats to make people invisible and to extract payment for the devil. People talked about cat conjuring and black cats were involved in numerous witchcraft trials. In Scotland, several witches confessed to trying to kill the King and Queen by killing and throwing a cat into the sea, thus creating a terrible tempest.

Cats were also used as a sacrifice—to ward off bad luck and to cure disease. One medieval practive was to wall a living cat in the foundation of a building to act as an amulet. In Eastern countries it was thought that burying a cat alive in a field would insure a fine harvest.

WORMS: In the main, cats are subject to two forms of parasitic worms: tapeworms and roundworms. Tapeworms may be seen in the cat's stool and around the anus, looking like grains of rice. Tapeworms cause irritability and digestive troubles but they seldom make the cat seriously ill. Treatment often is frustratingly slow and complete cure depends on the complete eradication of the carrier *fleas.*

Roundworms live in the cat's intestines or lungs and are not readily visible. The ones called ascarids are common in kittens, who sometimes acquire them while in the mother cat's womb. *Pot bellies* and *diarrhea* are symptoms. Treatment by drugs is usually effective. Hookworms are

Cats have always been associated with the occult. This one even has its own broomstick.

more serious. Infested cats are weak and anemic and may have bloody stools. Prompt veterinary treatment is imperative. Another type of roundworm, the lungworm, works its way into the cat's lung where it causes wheezing, sneezing, and coughing.

Less frequently cats get eye worms, heart worms, and muscle worms. The latter is called trichinosis and is caused by eating undercooked or raw pork.

If you suspect worms, take a sample of the cat's stool to your *veterinarian*. Do not try to treat the animal on your own. Wrong, or too strong medicine, can do much more harm than good.

WORSHIP OF CATS: The ancient Egyptians considered the cat a divine creature. Their goddess of fertility and feminity, Pasht, also known as Bast, Bubastis, and Ubastet, had a cat's face and features. If a cat died a violent death in the street, any passer-by had to prove his grief and innocence of being involved in the death by crying aloud and shedding copious tears. At home, if a cat died, the members of the household shaved their eyebrows in mourning. Once when the Persian army stole some cats, the Egyptians lost the battle rather than harm one precious cat hostage. Cats were also mummified and embalmed after death,

Porcelain cats in front of famous cat shrine Go-To-Ku-Ji in Tokyo.

sometimes with valuable cloth, precious jeweled collars, and the addition of artificial ears.

In Japan, cats are revered after death. In Tokyo they even have their own temple. On the temple altar, an assembly of bronze, paper, and porcelain cats greets the visitor, right paws raised to bring happiness and luck. Also in the temple is a statue of the Spirit-Cat, representing all the cats buried in the cemetery.

An Egyptian mummied cat in linen wrappings.

A bronze coffin for a cat.

The Goddess Bast with four kittens at her feet.

X Y Z

X-RAY: a special picture of the bones and internal structure, used by veterinarians to diagnose *hairballs*, broken bones, and other malfunctions, and to locate *foreign bodies* such as needles.

YEAST: rich in all the B vitamins important to growth and good appetite. It may be powdered and put in a cat's food or given in tablet form as most cats love it.

ZIBELINES: see *Burmese*.

ZOOPSYCHOLOGY: a popular term for the study of an animal's psyche and matters of its mind which in the cat are mysterious and complex.

BIBLIOGRAPHY

There are myriad cat books. Herein I am including only a sampling of books that were, to me, particularly informative, well-written and up-to-date, that span both sides of the Atlantic and that I think might be helpful to other cat owners and lovers. They vary in coverage, amount and kind of illustration and approach. One thing have in common: all are written by "cat people."

Note: Beyond informative books, cat books are unique in that they include art books, because the cat is so very intriguing to draw and photograph, philosophical and essay books, because the cat is such a springboard to thought and poetic imagination, and humorous books, because there is something so whimsical in the wonder of the cat. In other words, there are almost as many kinds of cat book as cats.

Ames, Felicia: *The Cat You Care For: A Manual of Cat Care*, N.Y., New American Library, 1968.

Carr, William H. A.: The Basic Book of the Cat. N.Y. Charles Scribner's Sons.

Cats Magazine: Pittsburgh, Pa., 1971–1973.

De Lys, Caludia & Rhudy, Frances: *Centuries of Cats*, Norwalk, Conn., Silvermine Publishers, 1971.

Dorland's Illustrated Medical Dictionary, Philadelphia, Pa., W.B. Saunders Co., 1965.

Fichter, George S. & Singer, Arthur B.: *Cats: A Golden Guide*, N.Y., Golden Press, 1973.

Gay, Margaret Cooper: *How to Live with a Cat*, N.Y., Simon and Schuster, 1971.

Henderson, G. N. & Mead, N. St. C.: *Cats: An Intelligent Owners' Guide,* London, Faber and Faber, 1966.

Henderson, G. N. & Coffey, D. J.: *The International Encyclopedia of Cats*, London, McGraw-Hill Book Company, 1973.

Ing, Catherine & Pond, Grace: *Champion Cats of the World*, London, George G. Harrap & Co. Ltd., 1972.

Kirk, Robert & Bistner, Stephen: *Handbook of Veterinary Procedures and Emergency Treatment*, Philadelphia, W. B. Saunders Co., 1969.

Mery, Fernand: *The Life, History and Magic of the Cat*, Paris, Editions Robert Laffont, 1966; N.Y., Grosset & Dunlap, Inc. 1967.

Schneider, Earl, editor: *Know Your Domestic and Exotic Cats*, N.Y., The Pet Library Ltd., (no date).

Schulberg, Howard, D.V.M.: *The Care of Your Cat*, N.Y., Pyramid Publishers, 1969.

Siegmund, O.H., editor: *The Merck Veterinary Manual*, Rahway, N.J., Merck & Co., 1967.

Tenent, Rose: *The Handbook of Cats and Their Care*, London, Arthur Barker Ltd., 1958.

Van der Meid, Louise Brown: *Cats*, Jersey City, TFH Publications, Inc., 1959.